FO...

on Literacy

G000292365

Starter Level
Teacher's Resource Book

Karina Law

Published by Collins
A division of HarperCollins*Publishers* Ltd
77–85 Fulham Palace Road
Hammersmith
London W6 8JB

www.**Collins**Education.com
On-line Support for Schools and Colleges

www.**fire**and**water**.com
Visit the book lover's website

First published 2001

© HarperCollins*Publishers* Ltd 2001

10 9 8 7 6 5 4 3 2

ISBN 0 00 711097 9

Karina Law asserts the moral right to be identified as the author of
this work.

Series editors: Barry and Anita Scholes
Editor: Caroline Pook
Design: Grasshopper Design Company
Cover image: Gary Hunter/Tony Stone Images
Scottish Curriculum referencing: Eleanor McMillan

Acknowledgements
The author and publishers would like to thank:
Pat O'Brien and all at English Martyrs RC Primary School, Liverpool;
John Foster for the extract from 'Here a Bear, There a Bear'
© 1996 John Foster.

Printed in Great Britain by Martins the Printers, Berwick-upon-Tweed

Contents

Focus on Literacy and the National Literacy Strategy

You will find in *Focus on Literacy* a strong support in the teaching of reading and writing within the context of a literacy hour. All the literacy objectives of the National Literacy Strategy may be covered by using the Big Book anthologies together with the Skills Masters, Read-along Book, Listen-along Cassette and the Teacher's Resource Book. Here, in one grand design, are sufficient teaching materials for five full literacy hours per week throughout the entire school year.

The aims of *Focus on Literacy*

The aims of *Focus on Literacy* are identical to those of the National Literacy Strategy: to develop each child's ability to read and write. It promotes their development by honing the literary skills necessary to meet the Range, Key Skills, and Standard English and Language Study of the National Curriculum Programmes of Study.

These skills are wide-ranging and specific:

- to read and write with confidence, fluency and understanding
- to use a full range of reading cues (phonic, graphic, syntactic, contextual) to self-monitor their reading and correct their own mistakes
- to understand the sound and spelling system, and use this to read and spell accurately
- to acquire fluent and legible handwriting
- to have an interest in words and word meanings, and to increase vocabulary
- to know, understand and be able to write in a range of genres in fiction and poetry, and understand and be familiar with some of the ways that narratives are structured through basic literary ideas of setting, character and plot
- to understand and be able to use a range of non-fiction texts
- to plan, draft, revise and edit their own writing
- to have a suitable technical vocabulary through which to understand and discuss their reading and writing
- to be interested in books, read with enjoyment, and evaluate and justify preferences
- to develop their powers of imagination, inventiveness and critical awareness through reading and writing.

The NLS framework and *Focus on Literacy*

The NLS teaching objectives for reading and writing are divided into three strands: text, word and sentence levels. Text level refers to comprehension and composition, word level to phonics, spelling and vocabulary, and sentence level to grammar and punctuation.

The literacy hour and *Focus on Literacy*

The NLS framework requires a literacy hour as part of school work each day. The literacy hour is designed to establish a common pattern for all classes and is carefully structured to ensure a balance between whole class and group teaching, as the diagram below shows.

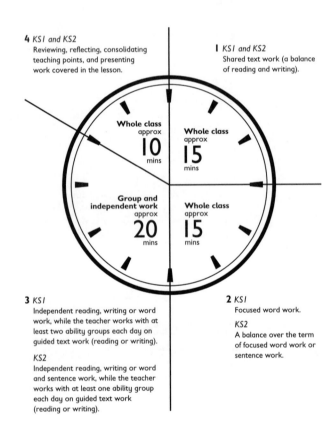

4 *KS1 and KS2*
Reviewing, reflecting, consolidating teaching points, and presenting work covered in the lesson.

1 *KS1 and KS2*
Shared text work (a balance of reading and writing).

Whole class approx **10** mins

Whole class approx **15** mins

Group and independent work approx **20** mins

Whole class approx **15** mins

3 *KS1*
Independent reading, writing or word work, while the teacher works with at least two ability groups each day on guided text work (reading or writing).

KS2
Independent reading, writing or word and sentence work, while the teacher works with at least one ability group each day on guided text work (reading or writing).

2 *KS1*
Focused word work.

KS2
A balance over the term of focused word work or sentence work.

Focus on Literacy Starter Level

Focus on Literacy Starter Level has been structured in a way that allows maximum flexibility. The different sections of the literacy hour may be taught as a whole, or in sections at different times of the day. This allows the freedom to plan the work with different groups throughout the day on guided reading and writing activities. Core activities are listed at the beginning of each unit. From these, the teacher may select activities appropriate for children of different levels of ability, and may decide how and when these are undertaken.

The high-quality texts of *Focus on Literacy* and the related activities directly meet the NLS objectives, and so relieve you of the burden of deciding what to teach. The teacher's notes support you in planning how to use the materials in your teaching.

Core activities

A list of core activities are set out at the beginning of each unit. These activities cover a range of abilities and skills and may be undertaken by children independently, at any time during the week, while you are working with groups on guided activities. They include opportunities for role-play, speaking and listening activities, pre-writing tasks for less able children, and extension activities for more able children.

Shared whole class time

Shared whole class time takes place during the first half of the literacy hour. It is divided into 15 minutes of shared text work (a balance of reading and writing) and 15 minutes of focused word and sentence work. This is the time when you can effectively model the reading/writing process with the children.

The NLS states that, in the early stages, in addition to guided reading books with a cumulative vocabulary, pupils should "be given a rich experience of more challenging texts" through shared reading. In shared reading, you can also help to extend reading skills in line with the NLS objectives: modelling the reading process, developing comprehension, and focusing on phonics and high frequency words.

The reading texts also provide ideas and structures for shared writing. Working with the whole class, you create the opportunity to model the writing process, teach grammar and spelling skills, demonstrate features of layout and presentation, and focus on editing and refining work. The shared writing will also be the starting point for guided and independent writing.

Guided/independent activities

The activities set out in this section, including the Skills Masters, may be undertaken with adult support or independently, depending on the nature of the task and each child's level of ability. In addition to these activities, teachers may select literacy tasks appropriate to the needs of individual children from the list of Core activities at the start of each unit.

Plenary

The plenary session is for reviewing, reflecting upon and consolidating teaching points, and presenting work covered. It is important to plan this essential element of the NLS in order to monitor children's progress and to highlight the teaching/learning points as necessary.

Phonics and handwriting

Focus on Literacy provides many opportunities for reinforcing the teaching of letter shapes and sounds, in harmony with whatever phonics programme you are currently using. Skills Masters focusing on all initial consonants, medial vowels and the digraphs *ch*, *sh* and *th* are included, to consolidate and extend children's knowledge of grapheme/phoneme correspondences.

The activities in *Focus on Literacy* offer many opportunities for the development of handwriting, while leaving you free to follow your school's own writing policy. Teaching suggestions and reinforcement activities are included, to support the teaching of letter formation. (Children should be supervised where possible, to ensure that they are using the correct sequence of movements.)

Using *Focus on Literacy*

The Big Book anthologies

There are three Big Book anthologies, each covering a term's work. These consist of carefully chosen texts for shared work on text, word and sentence levels. The extracts also provide the context for the activities. Each unit provides texts for a week's shared reading.

Each extract in the anthology is accompanied by a "To think and talk about" box to prompt and stimulate the children's responses.

Further teaching points and suggestions are given in the Teacher's Resource Book.

Read-along Book and Listen-along Cassette

The Read-along Book and Listen-along Cassette include many of the stories and poems featured in the Big Book anthologies. These resources provide children with a valuable opportunity to independently revisit and familiarise themselves with texts explored during shared reading.

Skills Masters

The Skills Masters offer a range of support materials designed to develop children's literacy skills. In addition to word level activities, they include a variety of writing frames and simple storyboards. Space is usually provided for emergent writing or to enable more able children to write a caption or sentence under each picture. Less able children who are still developing pre-writing skills will also benefit from using these sheets within a guided group setting to develop their story writing and sequencing skills orally. The Skills Masters are pitched at different ability levels, providing explicit opportunities for differentiation. It is not intended that all children complete every Skills Master; teachers should plan which core activities and which Skills Masters are appropriate for each ability group to undertake within each unit.

Children are likely to gain most benefit from the Skills Masters if they are used with support from the teacher or another adult, so that teaching points may be reinforced, letter formation may be supervised and group discussion stimulated. However, activities are also included which may be undertaken independently by children with just a small amount of introductory explanation.

High frequency words

The NLS lists 45 words that children are expected to recognise as "sight recognition words" by the end of the Reception year. Teachers are required to teach pupils to recognise these words in context when reading – particularly during shared text work with the whole class – and to reinforce them through other activities. The high frequency words that are featured in the Big Book anthologies are listed in the teacher's notes at the beginning of each unit. Flashcards featuring the 45 words for Reception are provided on Skills Masters 121–123. Suggestions are provided in the teacher's notes of different ways to use these flashcards, for example, by presenting them to the class for children to find within the shared text.

Word wheel and word slide

A word wheel and word slide are provided on Skills Masters 124 and 125. These may be used to investigate onsets and rimes explored with the teacher during focused word/sentence work sessions. Onset and rime combinations are suggested for the teacher to write on the wheel or slide, which may then be photocopied and constructed for each child within a group.

The Teacher's Resource Book

The Teacher's Resource Book comprises notes, photocopiable assessment masters and record-keeping sheets. It also outlines a basic approach to each unit in the Big Books and includes a reward certificate.

The teacher's notes and you

The teacher's notes will help you to use the *Focus on Literacy* material to the best advantage. The notes are arranged in five sections, each covering one literacy hour or day's teaching. These are further subdivided according to the literacy format: shared reading/shared writing work, focused word/sentence work, guided/independent work, and plenary. The structure allows flexibility for direct teaching to be spread across the day, and for guided and independent activities to be organised in the way that best suits the needs of the children.

A termly planning chart introduces each group of ten units. This chart lists the range of texts for that term, the text, sentence and word work that is explicitly covered, and the continuous work which will be part of your teaching throughout the term, such as practising reading and spelling strategies.

The teacher's notes for each text are organised to facilitate the literacy hour.

A *Key Learning Objectives* box lists the key literacy objectives covered in that week's work and a Resources box identifies the range of texts covered, details of the extracts, and the page references of all the components used in the unit.

The *High frequency words* featured in the Big Book anthologies are listed in the teacher's notes at the beginning of each unit.

Core activities are listed at the beginning of each unit. These activities are closely related to the key learning objectives and the shared reading text of each unit. Teachers may select from the activities for each ability group, appropriate to their stage of development, and organise how they are to be undertaken during the course of the week.

Details are given of any special *Preparation* you need to do for each unit, for example, providing illustrated dictionaries.

The *Shared reading* section lists teaching points and suggestions on how to explore the meaning of the text, in line with the literacy framework objectives. This entails: recognising printed and handwritten words in a variety of settings; recognising that words can be written down to be read again; correctly using terms about books and print; tracking text from left to right; exploring differences between spoken and written forms; re-telling and re-enacting known stories; understanding how story book language works; developing awareness of story structures; and experimenting with rhyming patterns established in stories and rhymes.

The texts often provide both structure and content for writing activities, and the context for many of the word and sentence level activities on the Skills Masters.

The *Shared writing* section offers guidance on how texts are composed. The text studied in earlier *Shared reading* sessions will provide the stimulus for this writing. Each shared writing activity is the starting point for subsequent guided/independent writing.

The *Focused word/sentence work* section offers appropriate teaching points and suggestions for teaching phonological awareness, phonics and spelling.

The *Guided/independent work* section introduces the unit's reading, writing, or word and sentence activities.

The *Plenary* section has suggestions for reviewing and reflecting upon the work covered, consolidating teaching points and presenting work.

A *Consolidation and extension* section has ideas and suggestions for follow-up activities, including reference to an additional Skills Master that may be used outside the literacy hour or as a homework sheet.

Record keeping

Record-keeping sheets are provided at the back of the Teacher's Resource Book. They feature a summary of the objectives at word, sentence and text level, each with a space for your comments.

Award certificate

A photocopiable award certificate is provided to reward significant individual achievements in literacy.

Basic approach to each day within each unit

The basic approach to each day in *Focus on Literacy* is as follows:

Day 1

- **Shared reading** using text in the Big Book.
- **Focused word/sentence work** based on the shared text.
- **Guided/independent word, sentence or text work** based on the shared text.
- **Plenary** session for which there are suggestions in the teacher's notes.

Day 2

- Further **shared reading** of a text.
- Further **focused word/sentence work** based on the text.
- **Guided/independent word, sentence or text work**.
- **Plenary** session, relating to the key learning objectives for Day 2.

Day 3

- **Shared writing** using the shared text as a model or stimulus.
- **Focused word/sentence work**, appropriate to the shared writing text.
- **Guided/independent writing task**, related to the shared writing activity.
- **Plenary** session, relating to the key learning objectives for Day 3.

Day 4

- Further **shared reading** of a text.
- Further **focused word/sentence work** based on the text.
- **Guided/independent word, sentence or text work**.
- **Plenary** session, relating to the key learning objectives for Day 4.

Day 5

- Further **shared reading** of a text.
- Further **focused word/sentence work** based on the text.
- **Guided/independent word, sentence or text work**.
- **Plenary** session, relating to the key learning objectives for Day 5.

Note: Core activities may be used in place of Guided/independent work for children for whom the Guided/independent task is inappropriate.

Work outside the literacy session

Further suggestions are provided for Consolidation and extension activities. These include an additional Skills Master, which may be used as a classroom resource or for homework. The Core activities listed at the beginning of each unit may be used at any time during the week for consolidation and extension. These include speaking and listening activities incorporating the Collins Starter Level Read-along Book and Listen-along Cassette, and opportunities for role-play, relating to the Big Book texts.

Big Book contents

STARTER LEVEL BIG BOOK A TERM I

STARTER LEVEL BIG BOOK B   TERM 2

STARTER LEVEL BIG BOOK C **TERM 3**

Read-along Book contents

Listen-along Cassette contents

SIDE 1	SIDE 2

Track		Track	
1	*Can Do*, Joyce Dunbar	13	*Alphabet Zoo*, Karina Law
2	*Ten Little Fingers*	14	*Catherine and the Lion*, Clare Jarrett
3	*Say!*, Dr. Seuss	15	*A Dark, Dark Tale*, Ruth Brown
4	*Doctor Foster / Rain, rain*	16	*The Baked Bean Queen*, Rose Impey
5	*What is the Sun?* Reeve Lindbergh	17	*It's Time for Lunch, Rosie!*, Tony Bradman
6	*Keith's Cupboard*, Michael Rosen	18	*Night Sounds*, Berlie Doherty
7	*The Grand Old Duke of York*	19	*Early Country Village Morning*, Grace Nichols
8	*O My Grand Old Grandpa York*, Lucy Coats	20	*The Gingerbread Man*, Karina Law
9	*The Enormous Turnip*, Karina Law	21	*Here a Bear, There a Bear*, John Foster
10	*Wet Play*, David Orme		
11	*Way Down South*		
12	*Lion*, Karina Law		

Skills Master checklist

	TERM 1	
Skills Master		
Unit 1	1	Pp is for princess
	2	Invitation
	3	Thank you card
	4	Bb is for beastie
Unit 2	5	Good days and bad days
	6	The best day ever
	7	Happy or sad?
	8	How do they feel?
Unit 3	9	Swimming
	10	Words with u
	11	What are they saying?
	12	Let's go swimming
Unit 4	13	The Seven Dwarfs
	14	Whose house?
	15	Goldilocks
	16	A letter
Unit 5	17	What can they do?
	18	I can ...
	19	I wish ...
	20	Who can do it?
Unit 6	21	Which letter?
	22	Noses, feet and tails
	23	I spy
	24	Label the dog
Unit 7	25	How many?
	26	If you're happy
	27	My hands ...
	28	Finger puppets
Unit 8	29	Ww is for weather
	30	Sun
	31	A rainbow
	32	Weather chart
Unit 9	33	New toys
	34	My best toy
	35	Tt is for toys
	36	In the toy shop
Unit 10	37	Kk is for kitten
	38	Cc is for cat
	39	Cats and rats
	40	Christmas presents

	TERM 2	
Skills Master		
Unit 11	41	Grandpa's teds
	42	Hh is for Humpty
	43	Humpty and Hugh
	44	Rhyming fun
Unit 12	45	Gg is for grandad
	46	Grandad's garden
	47	A letter to Grandad
	48	Grandad's plant
Unit 13	49	Words beginning with t
	50	The farmer's pets
	51	The Enormous Turnip
	52	Down on the farm
Unit 14	53	What shall we do today?
	54	Wet play
	55	Lost property
	56	This book belongs to me
Unit 15	57	Jj is for jungle
	58	Deep in the jungle
	59	ch is for chimpanzee
	60	Colours of the wild
Unit 16	61	Rr is for rabbit
	62	What do I need?
	63	Pets and vets
	64	Vv is for vet
Unit 17	65	a to z
	66	Aa is for apple
	67	Zz is for zoo
	68	Capital letters
Unit 18	69	Words with e
	70	A broken toy
	71	What is Granny knitting?
	72	An elephant
Unit 19	73	Mary had a little lamb
	74	Ll is for lion
	75	School days
	76	Word chains
Unit 20	77	Words with y
	78	My favourite season
	79	The four seasons
	80	Words beginning with s

Teacher's Notes

Starter Level
Term 1

HALF-TERMLY PLANNER

TERM I

Starter Level • Term I • Weeks I–5

SCHOOL _____ CLASS _____ TEACHER _____

		Phonetics, spelling and vocabulary	Grammar and punctuation	Comprehension and composition	Texts
Continuous work Weeks 1–5		WL 7, 10, 12, 13, 14	SL 1, 3	TL 1b, 1d, 2, 3, 11b, 11c, 11d, 11e, 12e, 13	**Range** **Fiction and poetry:** traditional, nursery and modern rhymes, chants, action verses, poetry and stories with predictable structures and patterned language **Non-fiction:** simple non-fiction texts, including recounts
Blocked work **Week**	**Unit**				**Titles**
I	I	WL 2a, 6, 8	SL 4	TL 6, 8, 9, 11a, 12a, 15	From *I Want My Dinner*, Tony Ross; *Say Please*, Michael Rosen
2	2	WL 2a, 4a, 6		TL 12c, 12d, 13, 14, 15	From *Good Days Bad Days*, Catherine and Laurence Anholt; From *I Feel Sad*, Brian Moses
3	3	WL 4a, 4b, 6, 9, 11	SL 2	TL 6, 11a 11f, 12c, 12d	From *Going Swimming*, Sarah Garland; *Animal Swimmers*, Karina Law
4	4	WL 2a, 2b, 4c, 9		TL 1c, 4, 5, 7, 9, 12d, 14, 15	*Seven of Everything* (illustrations); *A House in the Wood* (illustrations); From *Goldilocks*, Maggie Moore (Collins *Pathways*)
5	5	WL 4a, 4b, 6, 9		TL 6, 11f, 12c, 12d, 14a, 14b	From *Can Do*, Joyce Dunbar

SCHOOL _____ CLASS _____ TEACHER _____

	Phonetics, spelling and vocabulary	Grammar and punctuation	Comprehension and composition	Texts
Continuous work **Weeks 6–10**	WL 7, 10, 12, 13, 14	SL 1, 3	TL 1b, 1d, 2, 3, 11b, 11c, 11d, 11e, 12e, 13	**Range** **Fiction and poetry:** traditional, nursery and modern rhymes, chants, action verses, poetry and stories with predictable structures and patterned language **Non-fiction:** simple non-fiction texts, including recounts

Blocked work **Week**	**Unit**				**Titles**
6	**6**	WL 2a, 2b, 2c, 2d, 3a, 3b, 3c, 5, 8, 11	SL 4	TL 1c, 11f, 12b, 12c, 12d	*I Spy*, Barrie Wade (Collins *Pathways*)
7	**7**	WL 1a, 1b, 2a, 2b, 2c, 2d, 4a, 4b, 6, 9		TL 6, 10, 12a, 12c, 14	*Ten Little Fingers*, Anon; *Say!*, Dr. Seuss; *My Hands*, Anon
8	**8**	WL 1a, 1b, 2d, 2e, 4a, 5, 6, 11, 12b, 12c	SL 2	TL 6, 10, 11a	*Doctor Foster*, Anon; *Rain, rain, go away*, Anon; From *What is the Sun?*, Reeve Lindbergh; *No Rain, No Rainbow*, John Agard
9	**9**	WL 2a, 2b, 2c, 4b, 5, 6, 9, 11		TL 6, 11f, 12c, 15	*New Toys, Old Toys* (illustrations); *Keith's Cupboard*, Michael Rosen
10	**10**	WL 2d, 2e, 4a, 5, 8	SL 4	TL 4, 12b, 14	From *My Cat Mrs Christmas*, Adrian Mitchell; *Mrs Christmas*, Adrian Mitchell

TERM I

Focus on Literacy and the QCA Early Learning Goals

Early Learning Goals for communication, language and literacy	Unit									
	1	2	3	4	5	6	7	8	9	10
Help children to stick to the point and sensitively rephrase what they say to improve clarity and logic										
Demonstrate that the contributions of children are valued, and are used to inform and shape the direction of discussions										
Ask children to tell you about what they are going to do before they do it, and ask them to suggest possible outcomes										
Ask children to give reasons, further explanations or evidence for what they say										
Take an interest in what and how children think and not just what they know			C O N T I N U O U S			W O R K				
Encourage children to explain sometimes how things work in words rather than actions										
Show interest in and build on children's own observations about letters in words										
Read children's writing so that they understand that writing is an important way of communicating										
Intervene to help children hold a pencil effectively										
Set up collaborative tasks and help children to talk and plan together about how they will begin, what parts each will play and what materials they will need	●			●			●	●	●	
Foster children's enjoyment of spoken and written language in their play by providing interesting and stimulating opportunities	●		●	●		●	●	●	●	
Encourage children to predict possible endings to stories and events				●						
Encourage children to listen to each other and allow time for thinking, and for children to frame their ideas in words		●		●	●		●	●	●	
Encourage children to think about the effect of the words they use				●		●				
Model questions and explanations for children and help them expand on what they say			●					●	●	
Model fluent, phrased reading with big books and encourage children to predict, take over the telling and re-tell favourite stories	●	●	●	●	●	●	●	●	●	●
Provide opportunities for talking for a wide range of purposes		●	●	●	●	●	●	●	●	
Encourage children to experiment with words and sounds			●			●				
Encourage children to present and explain ideas to others and to expand on what they say			●		●		●	●	●	
Provide opportunities for children to participate in meaningful speaking and listening activities	●	●	●	●	●	●	●	●	●	
Encourage children to talk about how they feel		●			●					
Create a story with children, asking them to predict what will happen next		●								

Early Learning Goals for communication, language and literacy	Unit									
	1	2	3	4	5	6	7	8	9	10
Help children to identify patterns, draw conclusions, explain effect, predict and speculate								●		
Encourage children to explore and ask about the meanings of words				●				●		
Play interactive games to encourage children to listen for the sound at the end and then in the middle of words, and use the correct letter for the sound										
Model writing so that children can see spelling in action. Encourage children to apply their own knowledge of sounds to what they write	●	●	●	●	●	●	●	●	●	●
Sing the alphabet						●				
Discuss different versions of the same story				●						
Create group poems encouraging imaginative writing						●				
Model reading while children can see the text, maintaining natural intonation and observing punctuation	●	●	●	●	●	●	●	●	●	●
Create imaginary words to describe strong characters in stories and poems										
Help children identify the main events in a story. Encourage the children to enact stories and to use them as the basis for further imaginative play	●			●						●
Encourage children to add to their first-hand experience of the world through the use of books, other texts, and information and communication technology (ICT)			●					●	●	
Encourage children to use a range of reading strategies by modelling different strategies and providing varied texts through which that range can be used	●	●	●	●	●	●	●	●	●	●
Write stories, poems and non-fiction texts with children		●		●	●	●			●	
When writing, talk about what you are doing and why, and talk through some of your decision-making, such as what to write, choice of words, order. Continually re-read the writing to provide a good model for children when they write	●	●	●	●	●	●	●	●	●	●
Encourage children to use their ability to hear the sounds at various points in their writing		●			●				●	
Encourage children to re-read their writing as they write	●	●	●	●	●	●	●	●	●	●
Provide materials and opportunities for children to initiate the use of writing in their play, as well as creating purposes for independent and group writing	●				●				●	●
Give children extensive practice in writing letters, for example, labelling their work, making cards, writing notices	●	●	●	●	●	●	●	●	●	●
Continue writing practice in imaginative contexts	●	●	●	●	●	●	●	●	●	●
Use opportunities to help children form letters correctly, for example, when they label their paintings	●			●		●	●	●	●	

Unit 1 — Please and Thank You

Key Learning Objectives

TL6	To re-read frequently a variety of familiar texts, e.g. big books, story books
TL8	To locate and read significant parts of the text
TL9	To be aware of story structures, e.g. actions/reactions, consequences, and the ways that stories are built up and concluded
TL11	Through shared writing: a) to understand that writing can be used for a range of purposes, e.g. to send messages
TL12	Through guided and independent writing: a) to experiment with writing in role-play situations
TL15	To use writing to communicate in a variety of ways, e.g. lists, menus, greeting cards
WL2	Knowledge of grapheme/phoneme correspondences through: a) hearing and identifying initial sounds in words: *b, p*
WL6	To read on sight the 45 high frequency words to be taught by the end of YR
WL8	To read and write own name and explore other words related to the spelling of own name
SL4	To use a capital letter for the start of own name

Range:	Story with predictable structure; modern rhyme
Texts:	From *I Want My Dinner*, Tony Ross *Say Please*, Michael Rosen
Resources:	Starter Level Big Book A pp. 4–8 Skills Masters 1–4 and 121–123

High frequency words

a, and, for, go, I, my, no, said, the, to, you, we

Core activities

- Provide the children with props to re-enact the story extract from *I Want My Dinner*.
- Using modelling dough, ask the children to make food or objects beginning with *p* (for princess) or *b* (for beastie).
- Provide different invitation templates in the writing corner for the children to use to invite the princess to a party. More able children may use the sample invitations as models for designing their own invitations.
- Ask the children to make shopping lists for the princess' party, including foods beginning with *p*.
- Set up the role-play area for a party for the princess. Set a table for dinner and encourage the children to think of party games to play together after dinner.

Preparation

- Day 1: you will need an alphabet frieze and an illustrated dictionary or picture word book.
- Day 2: you will need a shopping basket and a box filled with items of shopping, most of which begin with *p*.

- Day 3: you will need the same resources as for Day 2; this time choose mostly items of shopping that begin with *b*.

DAY 1

Starter Level Big Book A pp. 4–7; Skills Master 1

Shared reading

- Begin by showing a picture of the Princess in this week's picture story and asking if any of the children have met her before in other stories, e.g. *I Want My Potty, I Want To Be, I Want a Sister*.
- Read the story to the class. Point to each word in turn and demonstrate that you are reading from left to right.
- Ask the class to think of times when they should remember to say "please" and times when they should say "thank you".

Focused word/sentence work

- Slowly say the words *princess, please, dinner, queen, potty, teddy, walk* and *beastie* one at a time. What initial sound can the children hear in each word?
- Say the words *princess, potty* and *please* again, emphasising the initial sound. Demonstrate how to write the letter that represents this sound and ask the children to draw it with a finger in the air and on the floor or table in front of them. Can they think of any other words that begin with *p*? Write them in a list on the board. Ask the children to find the letter *p* on an alphabet frieze and in an illustrated dictionary. Ask them to look for more words beginning with *p* to add to your list.

Guided/independent work

- Skills Master 1 focuses on the initial letter *p*.

Plenary

- Read *I Want My Dinner* once more, telling the class that you would like them to read some of the words for you. Pause at the word *please* each time it appears, for the class to supply the word, and again at the words *thank you*.
- Find out how children in your class who speak an additional language say "please" and "thank you" in those languages. The rest of the class can repeat each word.

DAY 2

Starter Level Big Book A pp. 4–7; Skills Master 2

Shared reading

- Talk in detail about the pictures in *I Want My Dinner*. Can the children tell you what the Princess is having for dinner? What are the cat and the Beastie having?
- Slowly read through the story again, encouraging the class to join in wherever they can.

Focused word/sentence work

- Ask the class to think of different types of food that a beastie might serve to a princess. Add an element of challenge by asking them to think of foods beginning with a particular sound, e.g. *p* for *pizza, pickles, pie, pineapple, potato, peppers, paella.*

- Ask a child to hold a shopping basket. Ask other children to identify items from your box (see Preparation) that begin with *p* and put them into the shopping basket.

Guided/independent work

- Skills Master 2 is a writing frame for an invitation from the Beastie to the Princess. Help the children to "read" the invitation and ask them to make suggestions about what to write in each space. Help them to complete the invitation.

Plenary

- Play an alliterative food game to develop the children's ability to discriminate initial sounds. Explain that the characters in this game only like foods that begin with their own initial sound. Ask them to listen out for the food in each list that does not begin with the same initial sound, for example:

  The Princess likes peas, pineapple, cabbage and pizza.
  The Beastie likes bananas, dumplings, biscuits and buns.

  Repeat the game using the names of children in the class, for example:

  Tamsin likes tomatoes, turnips, toffee and spaghetti.
  Callum likes cake, carrots, apples and crisps.

DAY 3

Skills Master 2 from Day 2

Shared writing

- Refer to the invitations the children completed on Day 2. Ask the children to help you write a reply on the board on behalf of the Princess. Encourage them to contribute as many ideas as they can to produce something along the following lines:

  Dear Beastie
  Thank you for inviting me to dinner on Sunday.
  It was very kind of you. I would love to come.
  Please can I bring Ted?

  Love from the Princess

  P.S. We don't like cabbage.

- Read the reply to the class and ask if there is anything that the children would like to add or change.

- Once everyone is happy with the reply you have written, encourage the class to "read" it with you again.

Focused word/sentence work

- Recite tongue twisters that focus on the letter *p* for *princess* or *b* for *beastie*, e.g. "Peter Piper picked a peck of pickled peppers" or "Betty Botter bought some butter".

- Help the children to compose more alliterative tongue twisters.

Guided/independent work

- Explain to the children that the Princess isn't very good at writing letters and would like them to write a reply to the Beastie's invitation on her behalf. (For most children, this will be an opportunity to practise their emergent writing.) You may like to provide key words for more able children to incorporate into their writing.

Plenary

- Invite as many children as possible to "read" their replies to the rest of the class.

DAY 4

Starter Level Big Book A pp. 4–7

Shared reading

- Read *I Want My Dinner* once more, encouraging the class to join in wherever possible now that they are becoming more familiar with the extract.

Focused word/sentence work

- Ask the children to locate the words in the text that are printed in capital letters. How should these words be read?

- Focus on the repeated line *Mmmmm* in the text. Point to the first example and ask the class to read it to you. Can they find this line repeated in the story extract? Ask the children to think of words beginning with the phoneme *m*.

- Make up alliterative sentences together using the phoneme *m*. Encourage the class to find different ways to finish the sentence "Monsters like to munch m ... " Repeat the sentences together.

Guided/independent work

- Ask children to write their own name, beginning with a capital letter, and draw or write the names of foods beginning with the same letter. (An illustrated dictionary would be useful for carrying out this activity.)

Plenary

- Play the alliterative food game that you played on Day 2. Remind the children that the characters in this game only like foods that begin with their own initial sound. Using different children's names, ask the class to listen out for the food in each list that does not begin with the same initial sound.

DAY 5

Starter Level Big Book A p. 8; Skills Master 3

Shared reading

- Read the poem by Michael Rosen on page 8, *Say Please*.

- What is the little boy trying to say? Have any of the children ever had trouble trying to find the right words to say?

Focused word/sentence work

- Ask the children to listen for the words that rhyme with *please*, as you re-read the poem.

- Give clues for the children to think of other words that rhyme with *please*, for example, "You need these to unlock doors" (*keys*); "these insects buzz and make honey" (*bees*).

Guided/independent work

- Ask the children to make a thank you card for someone they would like to say thank you to, using Skills Master 3. They might like to thank someone for making their dinner, taking them on an outing, inviting them to a party or being kind to them in some other way.

Plenary

- Give as many children as possible the opportunity to show their thank you cards to the rest of the class. Ask them to read any messages they have written or explain why they have chosen a particular person to send the card to.

Consolidation and extension

- Skills Master 4 focuses on the initial letter *b*.
- Ask the children to design a dinner menu fit for a princess, using words and pictures.
- Show the high frequency words used in the story to the class on flashcards (see Skills Masters 121–123). Ask the children to read the words and then locate them in the story.
- Read the full story of *I Want My Dinner* by Tony Ross. Invite the children to bring in any other books they have from the series about the Princess and share these with the class.

Unit 2 — Ups and Downs

Key Learning Objectives

TL12 Through guided and independent writing:
c) to write captions for pictures and drawings
d) to write sentences to match pictures or sequences of pictures

TL14 To use experience of simple recounts as a basis for independent writing, e.g. re-telling, substitution, extension, and through shared composition with adults

TL15 To use writing to communicate in a variety of ways, e.g. recounting their own experience

WL2 Knowledge of grapheme/phoneme correspondences through:
a) hearing and identifying initial sounds in words

WL4 To link sound and spelling patterns by:
a) using knowledge of rhyme to identify families of rhyming CVC words

WL6 To read on sight the 45 high frequency words to be taught by the end of YR

Range:	Simple non-fiction texts, including recounts
Texts:	From *Good Days Bad Days*, Laurence and Catherine Anholt
	From *I Feel Sad*, Brian Moses
Resources:	Starter Level Big Book A pp. 9–15
	Skills Masters 5–8, 121–123 and 124 or 125

High frequency words

a, all, and, are, at, can, day, for, I, in, it, like, me, my, on, to, we

Core activities

* Ask the children to find happy stories that they are familiar with for a class display entitled *They all lived happily ever after*. Write the titles of some of the children's chosen stories onto book jacket templates for the children to illustrate appropriately.

* Using your collection of objects (see Preparation and Day 1), give each child an opportunity to sort the items into hoops labelled *g* and *b*.

* Using magnetic letters, provide children with consonants to build words and non-words using the rime *-ad*.

Preparation

* Day 1: you will need two hoops, two cards for labels *g* and *b*, and a collection of objects beginning with *g*, e.g. glasses, a glove, glue, grapes, and *b*, e.g. a bag, a ball, a balloon, a banana, a bat, a bell, a book, a boot, a box, a brush and a button.

* Day 3: you may like to enlarge Skills Master 6 to A3 size to use as a writing frame for the children's ideas.

DAY 1

Starter Level Big Book A pp. 9–10; Skills Master 5

Shared reading

* Look at page 9 of Starter Level Big Book A. Talk about each picture in turn with the class. What is happening in each of the illustrations? Read the text, pointing to each word in turn. Ask the children to tell you about some of their good days and bad days.

* Turn to page 10. Ask the class to describe what is happening in each picture. Can the children spot two words that look the same? (*days*) Can anyone tell you what this repeated word is, using their knowledge of the text on the previous page? Read the two phrases to the children, pointing to each word as you do so.

* Encourage the class to tell you about their visits to a park or beach. How did they feel on these occasions? Children who have lost a pet may wish to talk about their experiences and feelings of sadness.

Focused word/sentence work

* Help the class to identify the initial phonemes in the words *good* and *bad*. Write the letter *g* on one card and *b* on another, and place them into two separate hoops. Show the class your collection of objects beginning with *g* and *b* (see Preparation). Ask the children to help you sort them into the correct hoops.

Guided/independent work

* Talk about Skills Master 5 with the children. Read the words and ask the children for suggestions about the sorts of things they could draw in each box, e.g. having a quarrel with a friend; receiving an award for an excellent piece of work. Encourage them to think of school-related experiences. There is a space under each picture for more able children to write a caption to describe their drawing or to copy the headings *good days* and *bad days*.

Plenary

* Invite some of the children to show their work to the class and explain what is happening in each picture.

* Write the phrase *good days* on one side of the board and *bad days* on the other. (Encourage the class to help you identify the phonemes to write the CVC word *bad*.)

* Play a game with the children where you describe a particular type of day, and the children decide whether it sounds like a good day or a bad day. For example: "It's raining and your friend isn't in school because he's not well" or "It's your birthday and your friend is coming to your house for tea." Ask them to point to the appropriate phrase as they "read" it to you. Encourage the children to have a go at describing a good or a bad day for the rest of the class to identify.

DAY 2

Starter Level Big Book A pp. 9–12

Shared reading

- Turn to pages 9 and 10 of Starter Level Big Book A and ask the class to remind you of what the words on the pages say. Emphasise that the words on the page remain constant, i.e. will always "say" the same thing.
- Turn to page 11. Do the children recognise any words on this page?
- Read the page to the class and talk about the pictures. Why is the little girl who is holding a doll fed up? What are the people in the queue waiting for? Are the children able to recognise the illustrations for birthday, summer holiday and Christmas?
- Read page 12 and talk about what is happening in each picture.

Focused word/sentence work

- Re-read page 11.
- Close the book and ask the children to tell you the initial phoneme in the word *fun*. Write *f* on the board and slowly repeat the word *fun*, encouraging the class to identify the second and third phonemes. You may like to ask higher ability children to come and write each phoneme in turn. (Check that they are forming the letters correctly as they model this to the rest of the class.)
- When you have finished, ask someone to find the word *fun* on page 11 and point to it. Investigate different onsets orally to find words that rhyme with fun, e.g. *b...*, *r...*, *s...*. Write these words in a list on the board. When the list is complete, help the class to read through the words they have made once again, prompting them with the initial sound if necessary.

Guided/independent work

- Ask children to think about and draw their idea of a fun day. Help them to write the caption "A fun day".

Plenary

- Choose different children to present and talk about their completed pictures. Ask children who have added further captions to their pictures to read them to the class.

DAY 3

Skills Master 6

Shared writing

- Tell the class that they are going to help you write about "The best day ever". This day could be based on real or imaginary experiences. It might include some of the following ideas.

  The best day ever would be a sunny day.
  In the morning we would visit the zoo.
  The zoo keeper would let us feed the elephants.
  For lunch we would have jelly and ice cream.
  In the afternoon we would fly by helicopter to the seaside.
  We would build an enormous sandcastle and have a picnic.

You may like to enlarge Skills Master 6 to A3 size to use as a writing frame for the children's ideas.

- Draw ideas from the children by questioning them further about their initial suggestions, for example, How would they travel there? What would they do there?
- Read their composition back to the class, pointing to each word as you do so. Find out if there is anything the children would like to add or change.

Focused word/sentence work

- Slowly say the word *best* so that the children can identify the separate phonemes. Ask them to help you write the word.
- Explore words and non-words that rhyme with *best*.

Guided/independent work

- Ask the children to record, with pictures and words, their idea of "The best day ever" on Skills Master 6. Help them to write simple captions to accompany their pictures.

Plenary

- Invite children to show and talk about their ideas of "The best day ever".

DAY 4

Starter Level Big Book A pp. 13–14; Skills Master 124 or 125

Shared reading

- Talk about the pictures on pages 13 and 14. What is happening in each one?
- Read pages 13 and 14 to the class, modelling the process of reading words one at a time, from left to right. Talk about the ideas. What makes the children feel sad?

Focused word/sentence work

- Ask the children to tell you the initial phoneme in the word *sad*. Write *s* on the board and slowly say the word *sad*, encouraging the class to identify the second and third phonemes. You may like to ask higher ability children to come and write each phoneme in turn. (Check that they are forming the letters correctly as they model this to the rest of the class.) Ask the children to find the word *sad* on pages 13 and 14. How many times can they spot the word and point it out to you?
- Orally, give the children different onsets to try putting together with the rime -*ad* to make a new rhyming word, e.g. *d...*, *h...*, *l...*, *m...*, *p...*. Write each new word they make on the board. When the list is complete, help the class to re-read the words they have made, prompting them with the initial sound if necessary.

Guided/independent work

- Give the children an opportunity to experiment with the rime -*ad*, using the word wheel or word slide on Skills Master 124 or 125. Ask more able children to write down the words they make.

Plenary

- Choose different children to show and talk about their ideas of "The best day ever".

DAY 5

Shared reading

- Re-read pages 13 and 14 before reading page 15 to the class. Encourage the children to talk about the things that they like to do to cheer themselves up when they are feeling sad. Who do they like to talk to when they feel upset? Do they have a special toy that makes them feel better? What else could they do to make themselves feel happy again?

Focused word/sentence work

- Ask the children to think of other words that are similar in meaning to sad, e.g. *upset, unhappy, miserable, fed up*.
- Challenge the class to recall as many words as they can, from Day 4, that rhyme with *sad*. Write these words in a list on the board and re-read them together once the task is complete.

Guided/independent work

- Skills Master 7 requires children to recognise the words *happy* and *sad* in order to join each picture to the correct label.

Plenary

- Talk about what is happening in each of the pictures on Skills Master 7. Ask the children to tell you what makes them feel happy or sad.
- Invite the children to tell you about any sad films they have seen or any sad stories they have heard.

Consolidation and extension

- Skills Master 8 requires children to choose the correct word to describe each picture and to complete simple sentences.
- Compile a class book called "The best days ever".
- Show the high frequency words used in the extracts to the class using the flashcards on Skills Masters 121–123. Ask the children to read the words and then find them in the story.
- Introduce regular "circle times" into the class routine, to give children an opportunity to share their experiences with the rest of the class. Pass an object around the circle, such as a pebble or soft toy, explaining that the children may either pass the object on to the next child, saying "pass" as they do so; or they may use the opportunity to talk to the class about a happy or sad time, or a special occasion.
- Sing the rhyme *If you're happy and you know it* together. Encourage the children to make up new lines.
- Talk about times to look forward to. Provide a class calendar for the children to write their names next to the dates on which they celebrate their birthdays.

Unit 3   Swimmers

Key Learning Objectives

TL6   To re-read frequently a variety of familiar texts, e.g. big books, information books, captions and own writing

TL11   Through shared writing:
a) to understand that writing can be used for a range of purposes, e.g. to inform
f) to apply knowledge of letter/sound correspondences in helping the teacher to scribe, and re-reading what the class has written

TL12   Through guided and independent writing:
c) to write labels or captions for pictures and drawings
d) to write sentences to match pictures or sequences of pictures

WL4   To link sound and spelling patterns by:
a) using knowledge of rhyme to identify families of rhyming CVC words
b) discriminating "onsets" from "rimes" in speech and spelling

WL6   To read on sight the 45 high frequency words to be taught by the end of YR

WL9   To recognise the critical features of words

WL11   To make collections of words linked to particular topics

SL2   To use awareness of the grammar of a sentence to predict words during shared reading and when re-reading familiar stories

Range:	Story with predictable structure Simple non-fiction text
Texts:	From *Going Swimming*, Sarah Garland *Animal Swimmers*, Karina Law
Resources:	Starter Level Big Book A pp. 16–21 Skills Masters 9–12 and 121–123

High frequency words

and, come, for, get, go, in, is, it, look, on, the, they, to

Core activities

• Set up an empty "paddling pool" in the role-play area for children to re-enact going swimming. Provide them with toy money, pretend tickets, towels, and a rubber ring or arm bands.

• Using magnetic letters and a paper clip tied to the end of a piece of string, set up a fishing game. The task is to "catch" all the *f* letters (for *fish* and *frog*). Alternatively, float plastic or foam letters in a water trough and ask the children to "fish out" all the *f* letters.

• Draw simple outlines of animal swimmers on an A4 sheet, e.g. *fish, frog, dolphin, duck, turtle, whale*. Photocopy a sheet for each child and ask them to write the initial sound of each animal within its outline. For less able children, write the initial letters on their sheet for them to select from and copy.

Preparation

• Day 3: you will need an enlarged copy of Skills Master 11 and Blu-tack.

• Day 4: you will need two hoops, a toy duck and frog (or a picture of each), and objects beginning with *d*, e.g. a die, a dish, a doll, a drum, and *f*, e.g. a feather, a flower, a fork.

• Day 5: prepare five flashcards for whole class use, featuring the following words: *duck, fish, frog, turtle, whale*.

DAY 1

Starter Level Big Book A pp. 16–19; Skills Master 9

Shared reading

• Begin by finding out about the children's own experiences of swimming. Do they like going swimming? Do they mind getting their faces wet?

• Talk about the illustrations on pages 16 and 17, and read the text, pointing to each word in turn.

• Ask the children with younger brothers or sisters whether they like going swimming. Are they frightened of the water?

• Read pages 18 and 19. Talk about the use of speech bubbles.

Focused word/sentence work

• Can the class find the word *please* on page 16? Remind them that this is a word they have met before. Can they tell you the name of the story and poem they have encountered this word in before? (Unit 1)

• Challenge the children to help you write the word *swim* on the board. Slowly say the word and ask them to tell you the first phoneme, *s*. Write this letter on the board and continue until all four phonemes have been identified and the word is complete. Can the children think of any other words that begin with *s*?

• Challenge more able children to think of other words that begin with *sw-*. (e.g. *swan, sweet, swing, switch*) Give the children clues to help them think of these words. Write each of the words that begin with *sw-* on the board under the word *swim*. Encourage the class to help you recall each word. Point to each word in the list as it is recalled.

Guided/independent work

• Skills Master 9 requires children to match captions to pictures based on today's shared reading text.

Plenary

• What special equipment do the children take with them when they go swimming? (e.g. *swimming trunks/costume, arm bands, float, swimming hat, goggles, towel*) Make a list of the children's suggestions on the board. Once it is complete, read through the list again.

DAY 2

Shared reading

- Look again at the illustrations on pages 16–19. Talk about what is happening.

- Read these pages again, omitting the last word of each line for the class to supply, e.g. "We're going ... " (*swimming*); "Three tickets ... " (*please*).

Focused word/sentence work

- Write the phrase *rub-a dub-dub* on the board. What do the children notice about these words? Can they recite the traditional rhyme, Rub-a dub-dub?

  Rub-a dub-dub,
  Three men in a tub,
  And how do you think they got there?
  The butcher, the baker,
  The candlestick-maker,
  They all jumped out of a rotten potato,
  'Twas enough to make a man stare.

- Investigate different onsets to make rhyming words and non-words, e.g. *bub, cub, fub, gub, hub, jub, lub, mub, nub, pub, sub, tub, wub*. Make a list of the words and non-words you have made.

- For fun, repeat the phrase *rub-a dub-dub*, replacing the final words each time with whichever word or non-word in the list you point to, e.g. *rub-a jub-jub*; *rub-a pub-pub*.

Guided/independent work

- Skills Master 10 focuses on CVC words containing *u*. An extension activity focuses on the rime -*ug*.

Plenary

- Recite the rhyme Rub-a dub-dub once more.

- Referring to Skills Master 10, ask the class to think of words that rhyme with *sun*. Write them in a list and re-read them together.

DAY 3

Shared writing

- Look through pages 16–19 with the children, focusing on the speech bubbles.

- Blu-tack an enlarged copy of Skills Master 11 to the board and ask the children to suggest words to write in each speech bubble. Once the class has agreed upon a phrase or sentence for each, write it in.

- Read through the speech bubbles together.

Focused word/sentence work

- Challenge children to help you write CVC words that they thought of on Day 2 that rhyme with *rub-a dub-dub*.

- Study other CVC words containing *u* that the children may be familiar with, e.g. *bun, but, fun, hug, hut, mug, rug*. Challenge children to read these words by themselves.

Guided/independent work

- Skills Master 11 provides children with an opportunity to write their own words, relating to the illustrations, in speech bubbles. Before they begin, ask the children to make suggestions about what each character might be saying. For children lacking in fine motor skills, use the sheet to stimulate discussion about what is happening and what the characters might be saying.

Plenary

- Invite children to show and read their independent work to the rest of the class.

- Ask the class to re-tell you, in sequence, the preparations involved in going swimming.

DAY 4

Shared reading

- Before you read the non-fiction text on pages 20–21, ask the children to think of different kinds of animals that can swim.

- Look at pages 20–21 in Starter Level Big Book A and ask the class to identify each of the animals that is shown there.

- Read the information on pages 20–21, pointing to the words as you read.

Focused word/sentence work

- Ask individual children to use a pointer to point out specific words in the text on pages 20–21 by drawing on their knowledge of the critical features of words, e.g. *Ducks, swim, Fish, Frogs, legs*.

- Place a duck in one hoop and a frog in another (see Preparation). Hold up each object in turn and ask the class whether it should go in the hoop with the frog or the duck.

Guided/independent work

- Using the resources you used in today's focused word work session, give each group an opportunity to sort the objects into the correct hoops.

Plenary

- Keeping the text from view, re-read pages 20–21 omitting the key words *ducks, fish, frogs*, etc. See if the class are able to tell you the animals you are reading about, from the context clues.

DAY 5

Shared reading

- Re-read the non-fiction text on pages 20–21, encouraging the children to join in if they are able to.

- Question the class about the information you have just read. How do fish swim? What sort of feet have ducks got? Can they think of any other animals that have webbed feet? (e.g. *geese, swans*) Which animal is the largest swimmer in the world?

Focused word/sentence work

- Using the flashcards you have made (see Preparation), divide the class into five groups and allocate one animal to each group. Familiarise each group in turn with their animal name, then hold up each card randomly. As each group recognises its animal name, they should indicate this by performing an action predetermined by you, e.g. quacking (ducks), croaking (frogs), holding their arms out in front to indicate size (whales).

Guided/independent work

- Ask the children to draw and write a caption about an animal swimmer of their choice.

Plenary

- Invite children to display and talk about their independent work to the rest of the class.

Consolidation and extension

- Skills Master 12 requires children to think about the items they might need to go swimming, providing a useful stimulus for group discussion. More able children could also write the initial sound next to each item.

- Show the high frequency words used in the extracts to the class on flashcards, using Skills Masters 121–123. Ask the children to read the words and then locate them in the text.

- Make a display of animal swimmers using pictures collected/drawn by the children. Add labels to the display as a whole class, including specialised words introduced in the non-fiction extract, such as *fin*, *webbed feet*.

Unit 4   Who Lives Here?

Key Learning Objectives

TL1   Through shared writing:
c) to understand and use correctly terms about books and print: *book, cover, title*

TL4   To notice the difference between spoken and written forms through re-telling known stories; to compare "told" versions with what the book "says"

TL5   To understand how story book language works and to use some formal elements when re-telling stories, e.g. "Once there was ... "; "She lived in a little ... "; "he replied ... "

TL7   To use knowledge of familiar texts to re-enact or re-tell to others, recounting the main points in correct sequence

TL9   To be aware of story structures, e.g. actions/reactions, consequences, and the ways that stories are built up and concluded

TL12   Through guided and independent writing:
d) to write sentences to match pictures or sequences of pictures

TL14   To use experience of stories as a basis for independent writing, e.g. re-telling, substitution, extension, and through shared composition with adults

TL15   To use writing to communicate in a variety of ways, e.g. letters

WL2   Knowledge of grapheme/phoneme correspondences through:
a) hearing and identifying initial sounds in words
b) reading letter(s) that represent(s) the sound(s): *a–z, ch, sh, th*

WL4   To link sound and spelling patterns by:
c) identifying alliteration in known and new words

WL9   To recognise the critical features of words, e.g. shape, length, and common spelling patterns

Range:	Stories with predictable structures
Texts:	*Seven of Everything* (illustrations) *A House in the Wood* (illustrations) From *Goldilocks*, Maggie Moore, Collins *Pathways*
Resources:	Starter Level Big Book A pp. 22–29 Skills Masters 13–16

High frequency words

and, a, the, in, of, you

Core activities

- Provide the children with props to re-enact the story extract from *Goldilocks*.
- Set up the role-play area to resemble the Three Bears' kitchen. Set a table for breakfast with three dishes and spoons. Include three chairs, preferably of different sizes. Put a sign over the entrance saying *Goldilocks keep out!*
- Make a collection of items, most of which begin with *g*, e.g. a game, glasses, a glove, glue, for the children to sort into a hoop labelled *g*.
- Collect different versions of the story of Goldilocks and the Three Bears with different illustrations. Allow the children time to look at the books independently and choose which illustrations they like best.

Preparation

- Day 3: write the following questions on a flipchart or board, leaving space after each line for extra words to be added:

  Who has been eating my porridge?
  Who has been sitting in my chair?
  Who has been sleeping in my bed?

- Day 4: you will need a traditional, printed version of the story of Goldilocks and the Three Bears. The children will need illustrated dictionaries or word books.

DAY 1

Starter Level Big Book A pp. 22–23; Skills Master 13

Shared reading

- Look at the house on page 22. Ask the children to describe what the house looks like on the outside. How many windows does the house have?
- Look at page 23. What can the children tell you about the inside of the house? How many beds are there? How many chairs are there around the table? Can anyone tell you who the house belongs to? Which famous story book character visited the Seven Dwarfs? Who was she trying to escape from?

Focused word/sentence work

- Look again at the external view of the Seven Dwarfs' house on page 22 of Starter Level Big Book A. Ask the class to describe it to you. Write down their words and phrases on a board or flipchart.
- Read the children's words and phrases back to them, pointing to the words as you do so. Are they able to make any further suggestions?
- Ask the class to tell you (if they have not already done so) the colours of the walls of the house, the door, the roof, the window frames and the roses.
- Repeat the phrase *red roses*. What do the children notice about the initial phoneme of these two words?
- Write the word *red* on the board. Can anyone find something inside the Seven Dwarfs' house that rhymes with *red*? Rub out the onset *r* in *red*. Ask the class what sound you should put in its place to make the word *bed*. Who can show you what the letter that makes that sound looks like? (Invite a child to write the letter in the correct place on the board.)

Guided/independent work

- Ask the children to colour the picture of the outside of the Seven Dwarfs' house, following the specific instructions on Skills Master 13. Read through these instructions together before the children begin. More able children could label parts of the house or write a sentence about it.

Plenary

- Ask the children to swap their pictures of the Seven Dwarfs' house with a friend. Ask the friend to check that the instructions have been followed correctly and that their friend has included seven windows. Invite any children who have written a sentence about their house to read it aloud to the rest of the class.

- Ask the children who are familiar with the story of Snow White and the Seven Dwarfs to re-tell it to the rest of the class.

DAY 2

Starter Level Big Book A pp. 24–25; Skills Master 14

Shared reading

- Talk about the house on pages 24 and 25. Can the children tell you who lives there?

- How many bowls of porridge are on the kitchen table? Which of the beds belongs to Baby Bear? Which of the beds belongs to Mummy Bear? Who is going to visit this house while the bears are out walking in the wood?

Focused word/sentence work

- Look at the objects inside the house on page 25. Who can find something in the Three Bears' house beginning with *b, l, j, m, s, r* and *ch*? (e.g. *bed, lamp, jug, mop, sink, rug* and *chair*) As the children find each item in turn, ask them to finger trace the shape of the initial letter as you draw it on the board and repeat the sound together. Challenge a more able child to show you how the phoneme *ch* is written. Who can think of other words beginning with this sound?

Guided/independent work

- Skills Master 14 is a matching activity to help develop observation skills. Children are required to draw a line connecting each word with the matching object in the Three Bears' house.

Plenary

- Look at the different sizes of the porridge bowls, chairs and beds. Ask the children: "Who sleeps in the biggest bed?"; "Who sits on the medium-sized chair?"; "Who does the smallest bowl of porridge belong to?" etc.

- Ask the children if they can think of any other words similar in meaning to *small* e.g. *little, tiny*. Can they think of any words similar in meaning to big? (e.g. *large, enormous, huge*) Ask them to think of different examples of small things, e.g. an ant, a paper clip, a button; and big things, e.g. a mountain, a castle, a lorry.

DAY 3

Starter Level Big Book A pp. 26–29; Skills Master 15

Shared writing

- Introduce the story board that begins on page 26 of Starter Level Big Book A. Can the children tell you the title of the story?

- Using the pictures, encourage the class to retell the story of Goldilocks and the Three Bears collectively. Even those children who had not heard the story prior to this week should by now be reasonably familiar with it. Encourage the children to use some of the formal elements of story telling, e.g. "Once there was ... "; "They lived in a little ... "; "he replied ... ".

- Why did Goldilocks not like Daddy Bear's and Mummy Bear's porridge? What was wrong with their chairs and beds? How do the children think the bears felt when they discovered there had been an intruder in their home? How must Goldilocks have felt when she was discovered sleeping in Baby Bear's bed? Why did she run away?

- Write key words and simple phrases or sentences on the board as children contribute their ideas.

Focused word/sentence work

- Divide the class into three groups: baby bears, mummy bears and daddy bears. Role-play the end part of the story when the Three Bears return from their walk and discover that an intruder has been in their home. As you reach the words spoken by each of the bears, point to them on the board. Ask each group to "read" the words spoken by the bear they are role-playing.

- The "baby bears" might like to add a few words at the end of their lines, e.g. "... and has eaten it all up". Write these extra words after the relevant lines on the board.

Guided/independent work

- Skills Master 15 requires children to sequence pictures from the story of Goldilocks and the Three Bears. Children who are more able could be encouraged to add captions.

Plenary

- Discuss with the whole class the correct sequence for Skills Master 15. Ask the children to give their suggestions for appropriate captions under each picture.

DAY 4

Starter Level Big Book A pp. 26–29

Shared reading

- Using the pictures on pages 26–29, encourage the class to briefly re-tell the story of Goldilocks and the Three Bears collectively once more. Read a traditional version of the story from a book to the class, and discuss how their oral version compares with the printed version. Draw the children's attention to some of the formal elements of storytelling in the printed version, e.g. "Once there was ... "; "They lived in a little ... "; "he replied ... ".

Focused word/sentence work

- Write the letter *g* on the board and ask the children to finger trace the shape in the air and on a surface near to them. Ask a volunteer to write a capital *G* for *Goldilocks* on the board.
- Ask the children to think of other words that begin with *g*, e.g. *game, gap, garden, gate, glasses, glove, glue, goal, goat, good, goose, gorilla, green, guitar*. Give them clues to some of these words if they are unable to think of them for themselves.

Guided/independent work

- Ask the children to draw things beginning with *g* using an illustrated dictionary or word book. More able children could also label each picture, by referring to their dictionary or word book.

Plenary

- Ask the class to think about the character of Goldilocks and suggest words to describe her, e.g. *naughty, pretty, young, frightened, cheeky*.
- What do the children think Goldilocks told her mother, when she arrived home after visiting the Three Bears' house? Explore their ideas through role-play.

DAY 5

Starter Level Big Book A pp. 26–29

Shared reading

- Explore different sections of the story of Goldilocks and the Three Bears through role-play, using the story board on pages 26–29.

Focused word/sentence work

- Ask the class to tell you again the phoneme they can hear at the beginning of Goldilocks' name. Can they remember a few other words that begin with *g*?

- Tell the children that, apart from porridge, Goldilocks only likes things that begin with *g*. Ask the questions, such as:

  Does Goldilocks like grapes?
  Does Goldilocks like goats?
  Does Goldilocks like snakes?

Guided/independent work

- Write the title "Goldilocks and the Three Bears" on a book jacket template and photocopy for each child. Ask them to design a cover, drawing upon their knowledge of the story. If possible, show them various different covers for different versions of the story. Introduce the terms *book*, *cover* and *title*.

Plenary

- Make up silly sentences together using words beginning with *g*, e.g. "I once met a gorilla wearing green gloves and glasses"; "My gran has a garden full of goats and geese."

Consolidation and extension

- Ask the children to write a "sorry" letter or make a card for the Three Bears on behalf of Goldilocks. Skills Master 16 may be used for this purpose. Talk about language specific to letter writing. Encourage the children to think of different ways to end a letter, e.g. *from, with love, best wishes*.

- Read and compare different versions of the traditional story of Goldilocks and the Three Bears or Snow White and the Seven Dwarfs.

Unit 5 Can Do

Key Learning Objectives

TL6 To re-read frequently a variety of familiar texts, e.g. big books, taped stories with texts, captions, own and other children's writing

TL11 Through shared writing:
f) to apply knowledge of letter/sound correspondences in helping the teacher to scribe, and re-reading what the class has written

TL12 Through guided and independent writing:
c) to write labels or captions for pictures and drawings
d) to write sentences to match pictures or sequences of pictures

TL14 To use experience of simple recounts as a basis for independent writing

WL4 To link sound and spelling patterns by:
a) knowledge of rhyme to identify families of rhyming using CVC words
b) discriminating "onsets" from "rimes" in speech and spelling

WL6 To read on sight the 45 high frequency words to be taught by the end of YR

WL9 To recognise the critical features of words

Range:	Poetry and stories with predictable structures and patterned language
Text:	From *Can Do*, Joyce Dunbar
Resources:	Starter Level Big Book A pp. 30–34 Skills Masters 17–20, 121–123 and 124 or 125 Listen-along Cassette Track 1 and Read-along Book pp. 4–8

High frequency words

a, and, are, at, big, can, cat, get, I, in, is, like, my, of, see, the, to, you

Core activities

- The Listen-along Cassette (Track 1) and Read-along Book (pp. 4–8) feature this unit's extract from *Can Do* by Joyce Dunbar. Give each child an opportunity to use these resources to consolidate this week's reading skills and to reinforce the high frequency words that appear in the text.

- Set a variety of tasks around the room, e.g. "Do the alphabet jigsaw." Next to each task leave a class list entitled, for example, "Who can do the jigsaw?" Ask the children to find and put a tick against their names once they have successfully completed the task.

- Provide different award certificate templates in the writing corner for the children to fill in for themselves or other children, in recognition of a particular achievement, such as learning to tie shoe laces, being able to count to twenty, or being the first to dress themselves after a PE lesson. More able children may use the sample certificates as models for designing their own certificates. (You may like to include the photocopiable certificates on page 122 as one example.)

Preparation

- Day 1: prepare three large flashcards featuring the words *hop*, *skip* and *jump*.
- Day 4: You will need the high frequency words included in this unit's extract (see left), using the flashcards featured on Skills Masters 121–123.

DAY 1

Starter Level Big Book A pp. 30–31; Skills Master 17

Shared reading

- Introduce this week's extract from *Can Do* by Joyce Dunbar, which begins on page 30. Read pages 30 and 31, using the pictures to make sense of words such as *bird*, *cat* and *slide*.
- Find out who in the class can hop, skip, jump and slide down a slide.
- Ask the children to tell you about anything that they wish they could do.

Focused word/sentence work

- Slowly say the words *hop*, *skip* and *jump* and encourage the class to tell you the separate phonemes in each word. As each phoneme is identified, write the corresponding letter on the board. Then erase each word in turn and challenge children to rewrite them.

Guided/independent work

- Skills Master 17 requires children to label illustrations depicting different actions, using CVC and CCVC words.

Plenary

- Using the flashcards (see Preparation) familiarise the children with the words *hop*, *skip* and *jump*. Teach them an action to correspond with each word, then display the words at random. Ask the children to perform the corresponding action once they have recognised the word you are showing.

DAY 2

Starter Level Big Book A pp. 30–32; Skills Master 124 or 125

Shared reading

- Re-read pages 30 and 31, pausing for the class to supply the words *hop*, *skip* and *jump*; *cat* and *tin*.
- What can the children see in the top right corner on page 32? What do they think is in the bag she is holding? What is the boy doing? Read page 32.
- Find out who in the class can blow bubbles. Can anyone whistle a tune? Spin a web? Catch a tooth fairy?

Focused word/sentence work

- What do the children notice about the words *CAN'T* and *CAN*? Talk about the times when we use capital letters, e.g. at the beginning of a name or to start a sentence. Explain the purpose of capital letters in this instance. Re-read page 32 together, placing greater emphasis on these words.

- Close the book and encourage the class to help you write the phrase *spin a web* on the board by listening as you slowly say the words and then identifying each phoneme.
- Cover *sp* in the word *spin* and ask the children to read the high frequency word that remains. Investigate different onsets to build non-words and words that rhyme with spin, e.g. *bin, din, fin, pin, tin, win*.

Guided/independent work

- Give each child an opportunity to investigate the rime *-in* using the word wheel or slide on Skills Master 124 or 125. Challenge more able children to write down the words they make.

Plenary

- Find out what words the children were able to make using the rime *-in*. Write them in a separate list and ask the class to help you read them back.
- Write the sentence opener *I can ...* on the board and ask the class to read it to you. Encourage the children to think of different ways to finish the sentence (orally).

DAY 3
Skills Master 18

Shared writing

- Building on Day 2's plenary work, ask the children to complete the sentence *I can ...* , this time writing down some of their ideas.

Focused word/sentence work

- Focus on the high frequency words *I* and *can*. What do the children notice about the word *I*? Remind them that *I* as a word on its own is always a capital letter.
- Look at the word *can*. Experiment with other onsets to build rhyming words and non-words, e.g. *fan, man, pan, ran, tan, van*.

Guided/independent work

- Skills Master 18 is a writing frame for children to explore different ways of completing the sentence *I can ...* .

Plenary

- Invite children to show their pictures and read their completed sentences to the rest of the class.

DAY 4
Starter Level Big Book A pp. 33–34;
Skills Masters 121–123

Shared reading

- Can the children recall all of the things that the child in this week's extract can do?
- Read pages 33 and 34. What is the boy doing in each of the pictures on page 34?
- What is the highest number that your class can think of? Who can write in straight lines? Who likes to read scary stories? Who can paint a lovely funny picture? Who can cut out paper chain people? Who can turn head-over-heels? Who can get dressed all by themselves?

Focused word/sentence work

- Using the high frequency word flashcards (see

Preparation), hold up the words that appear in this week's extract in turn and ask the class to read them to you. Challenge individual children to locate them in the story.

Guided/independent work

- Using foam, plastic or magnetic letters, ask the children to make words and non-words ending in *-an*.

Plenary

- Find out what words the children were able to make using the rime *-an*. Write them in a list and ask the class to help you read them back.

DAY 5
Starter Level Big Book A pp. 30–34; Skills Master 19

Shared reading

- Re-read the whole of this week's extract with the class, encouraging them to read as much as possible by themselves.

Focused word/sentence work

- Write the words *I wish ...* on the board. Ask the children to read these words. Cover the rime *-ish* and ask the children to identify the first phoneme in the word *wish*. Then ask them to tell you the second phoneme. Cover *wi* and see if they can tell you the phoneme represented by the letters *sh*.
- Can anyone think of an animal that lives in water that ends with *sh*? (fish) Give clues to other words ending in *sh*, e.g. *crash, dish, finish, wash*.

Guided/independent work

- Ask the children to write a sentence beginning with the words *I wish ...* , using Skills Master 19. Point out the thought bubble to the children and ask them to draw a picture in the bubble to show their wish coming true.

Plenary

- Sit the children in a circle and pass an object such as a pebble or a favourite toy around the circle. Ask each child to finish the sentence *I wish ...* before passing the object on to the next child. Children who are unable or unwilling to complete the sentence can say "pass" before passing the object on to the next child. Repeat this activity using the sentence opener *I can ...* .

Consolidation and extension

- Skills Master 20 will extend children's reading skills and reinforce the high frequency words: *can, he, she* and *they*.
- Use Skills Master 124 or 125 to investigate the rime *-an*.
- Show the children how to cut out paper chain people. Use this as an opportunity to develop the children's listening skills, and see how effectively they are able to follow your instructions during a guided group session.
- Make a class photo album, featuring every child in the class demonstrating something that they feel proud to be able to do, e.g. running, reading, climbing, painting, playing the recorder, tying shoe laces, dancing, swimming. Entitle the album "We can ... ". Help each child to write a caption to go underneath his or her photograph.

Unit 6 I Spy

Key Learning Objectives

TL1 Through shared reading:
c) to understand and use correctly terms about books and print: *letter*

TL11 Through shared writing:
f) to apply knowledge of letter/sound correspondences in helping the teacher to scribe, and re-reading what the class has written

TL12 Through guided and independent writing:
b) to write their own names
c) to write labels or captions for pictures and drawings
d) to write sentences to match pictures or sequences of pictures

WL2 Knowledge of grapheme/phoneme correspondences through:
a) hearing and identifying initial sounds in words
b) reading letter(s) that represent(s) the sound(s): *a–z, ch, sh, th*
c) writing each letter in response to each sound: *a–z, ch, sh, th*
d) identifying and writing initial and dominant phonemes in spoken words

WL3 Alphabetic and phonic knowledge through:
a) sounding and naming each letter of the alphabet in lower and upper case
b) writing letters in response to letter names
c) understanding alphabetical order through alphabet books, rhymes, and songs

WL5 To read on sight a range of familiar words, e.g. children's names, captions, labels, and words from favourite books

WL8 To read and write own name and explore other words related to the spelling of own name

WL11 To make collections of personal interest or significant words and words linked to particular topics

SL4 To use a capital letter for the start of own name

Range:	Simple non-fiction text
Text:	*I Spy*, Barrie Wade, Collins *Pathways*
Resources:	Starter Level Big Book A pp. 35–38 Skills Masters 21–24

High frequency words

am, and, cat, I, my

Core activities

- Find pictures of animals beginning with the first six letters of the alphabet, e.g. *ant, bear, cat, dog, elephant, frog*. Give the children plastic or foam letters for *a–z* to place on the pictures. Challenge them to sequence the pictures in alphabetical order (provide an alphabet line or suggest that they use an alphabet frieze as a point of reference).

- Make a collection of alphabet books for the children to look at independently.

- Draw an outline of a cat or dog on a large sheet of card (or enlarge the dog on Skills Master 24). Make, or cut out, labels saying *eye, fur, nose, paw, tail, whiskers, ear* and *claw*. Set a task for pairs or small groups of children, to place the labels on the drawing in the appropriate places. (Most children will need to refer to the text in Starter Big Book A for help in completing this activity.)

Preparation

- Day 2: prepare a tray with the following items: a fan or a toy frog, a nut or a nail, a pen or pasta, a tin or a teddy, a wand or a watch, an egg or an envelope, crisps or a toy cat.

- Day 3: the children will need illustrated dictionaries.

- Days 3 and 4: you will need foam, plastic or magnetic letter shapes or letter cards (*a–z*).

- Day 4: you will need Post-it Notes, or something similar.

DAY 1

Starter Level Big Book A pp. 35–36; Skills Master 21

Shared reading

- Introduce this week's text, by Barrie Wade. Read pages 35–36, pausing for the children to identify the letters *f, n, p* and *t*.

- Ask the class to think of other animals that have fur. Can they think of other animals that have paws? Can they name animals that have tails?

Focused word/sentence work

- Play I Spy with the children for each of the letters *f, n, p* and *t*. Ask the children to look around the room for objects beginning with each of these letters.

- Model how to form each of these letters on the board. Choose children to demonstrate the correct way to write each letter. Ask the class to finger trace each letter in the air and on a nearby surface.

Guided/independent work

- Skills Master 21 requires children to discriminate and write the initial letter of each item depicted. Less able children could simply join up the pairs that begin with the same phoneme.

Plenary

- Play a game to develop the children's listening skills. Give clues to different animals for the class to guess, e.g. "I am large and grey, with four legs, a long trunk and two white tusks."

DAY 2

Starter Level Big Book A pp. 37–38; Skills Master 22

Shared reading

- Read pages 37 and 38, pausing for the children to identify the letters *w, e* and *c*.

Focused word/sentence work

- Focus briefly on the word *eye*. Acknowledge that in the word *eye*, the initial *e* is not making its regular sound.

What sound does the letter *e* usually make? Challenge the class to think of words beginning with the short vowel *e*, e.g. *egg, elephant, envelope*.

- Challenge the children to think of other words beginning with *w* and *c*.

Guided/independent work

- Skills Master 22 requires children to join up different body parts to the correct animal.

Plenary

- Play I Spy using your tray of objects (see Preparation). As a child identifies an object beginning with *f, n, p, t, w, e* or *c*, give them the object and write the initial letter on the board. When the tray is empty, ask each child holding an object to point out the corresponding initial letter on the board before returning the item to the tray.

DAY 3

Starter Level Big Book A p. 38

Shared writing

- Re-read the last few lines on page 38 together:

  Eye and fur,
  nose and paw,
  tail and whiskers,
  ear and claw.
  What am I?
  cat

- Decide on an animal and make up another "riddle" together for the children to take home and try on their families and friends. Begin with a simple list of features, such as stripes, teeth and claws. Then encourage the class to contribute words to describe these features to make the riddle more interesting.

  For example:

  Orange and black stripes,   Tail, trunk, and tusks,
  sharp teeth and claws.   four strong legs.
  What am I?   What am I?
  tiger   **elephant**

  Under water swimmer,
  shiny scales and flapping tail.
  What am I?
  fish

(The children may find this activity easier if you are able to provide a picture of the animal you are writing about, to stimulate ideas.)

Focused word/sentence work

- Using letter shapes or letter cards, hold up each letter in turn, starting with *a*. See who can think of an animal beginning with each letter, e.g. *ant, bear, cat, dog*. Give each letter to the child who first thinks of an animal. Put aside any letters that the class cannot think of animals for, then working through the alphabet from *a* to *z*, collect each letter from the children, asking them to recall the animal they thought of as you do so. Who collected the most letters?

Guided/independent work

- The children may choose one of the animals you worked on as a whole class and draw it. Ask them to try labelling

its different body parts. You may like to provide children with an animal outline and simple labels to stick on their animal.

- Alternatively, more able children may prefer to choose an animal and write simple clues about it, building on the shared writing experience. They could present their composition on a folded sheet of paper, which will open like a greetings card; ask them to write their clues on the outside and, on the inside, draw a picture of their animal and write its name. Encourage the children to look for their animal in an illustrated dictionary and copy its name.

Plenary

- Referring to the riddles you wrote together as a class, focus on the words that refer to animal body parts, e.g. *teeth, claws, tail, trunk, tusks, legs, scales, tail*. Which of these do humans have? Which parts do humans not have? Encourage the children to point to the relevant words as they answer your questions.

DAY 4

Starter Level Big Book A pp. 35–38; Skills Master 23

Shared reading

- Re-read pages 35–38 together.

Focused word/sentence work

- Using Post-it Notes or something similar, turn away from the class and cover the letters *f, n, p, t, w, e* and *c*. Challenge the class to re-read pages 35–38 together and tell you the letters that are covered up. Invite volunteers to write each letter over the Post-it Note once the class has agreed upon what it is.

- Peel away each Post-it Note in turn to confirm whether or not the children were correct.

Guided/independent work

- Skills Master 23 presents a game of I Spy. The children are required to identify initial letters for a pig's snout (also accept *n* for nose), a tail and trotters (accept *f* for feet).

Plenary

- Repeat the alphabet game you played during the focused word work session on Day 3.

- Sing the alphabet together.

DAY 5

Starter Level Big Book A pp. 35–38

Shared reading

- Encourage the class to re-read pages 35–38 with as little help as possible.

Focused word/sentence work

- Play "I spy someone whose name begins with ...". As each name is successfully guessed, write it on the board. What do the children notice about the initial letters of each name? Remind them that names always start with a capital letter.

Guided/independent work

- Give each child an A5 piece of card. Instruct them to write their names as neatly as possible, making sure that they begin with a capital letter. Ask them to decorate their name card with an animal that begins with their initial. Once completed, the cards may be used to form a class display, or as a label on the front of a book or folder. Alternatively they may be taken home to be used as a bedroom-door name plaque.

Plenary

- Collect the children's name cards. Hold each one up in turn for the class to read, using the initial letter as a clue. The child whose name it is should remain silent when his or her card is presented.

Consolidation and extension

- Skills Master 24 reinforces the vocabulary introduced in this week's shared text. Children are required to label the different parts of a dog.
- Using toy animals, such as a soft toy rabbit, or pictures of animals, play I Spy, referring to different parts of the toy, e.g. *tail*, *nose*, *whiskers*, *fur*.

Unit 7 Fingers and Thumbs

Key Learning Objectives

TL6   To re-read frequently a variety of familiar texts, e.g. big books, taped stories with texts, poems, captions

TL10 To re-read and recite rhymes with predictable and repeated patterns and experiment with similar rhyming patterns

TL12 Through guided and independent writing:
a) to experiment with writing in a variety of play, exploratory and role-play situations
c) to write captions for pictures and drawings

TL14 To use poems as a basis for independent writing, e.g. substitution, extension, and through shared composition with adults

WL1   To understand and be able to rhyme through:
a) recognising, exploring and working with rhyming patterns, e.g. learning nursery rhymes
b) extending these patterns by analogy, generating new and invented words in speech and spelling

WL2   Knowledge of grapheme/phoneme correspondences through:
a) hearing and identifying initial sounds in words
b) reading letter(s) that represent(s) the sound(s): *h*
c) writing each letter in response to each sound: *h*
d) identifying and writing initial and dominant phonemes in spoken words

WL4   To link sound and spelling patterns by:
a) using knowledge of rhyme to identify families of rhyming CVC words
b) discriminating "onsets" from "rimes" in speech and spelling

WL6   To read on sight the 45 high frequency words to be taught by the end of YR

WL9   To recognise the critical features of words

Range:	Traditional and modern rhymes; action verses
Texts:	*Ten Little Fingers*, Anon *Say!* from *One fish, two fish, red fish, blue fish*, Dr. Seuss, Collins *My Hands*, Anon
Resources:	Starter Level Big Book A pp. 39–44 Skills Masters 25–28, 121–123 and 124 or 125 Listen-along Cassette Tracks 2 and 3, and Read-along Book pp. 9–13

High frequency words

all, and, at, can, he, I, is, like, look, me, my, on, see, they, this, to, up, you

Core activities

- Give each child an opportunity to revisit this unit's rhymes using the Listen-along Cassette (Tracks 2 and 3) and Read-along Book (pp. 9–13). Encourage them to follow the text as they listen to each rhyme.

- Provide glove or finger puppets for the children to re-enact stories that are familiar to them with their hands.

- Using a word wheel or slide (Skills Master 124 or 125), provide an opportunity for children to investigate the rime *-ap*. Children who are already confident working with CVC words could investigate the rime *-and* to find words that rhyme with *hand*.

- Give every child an opportunity to make a hand print using paint. Ask them to label their picture *My hand*.

- Ask each child to write the letter *h* in lower and upper case using a finger tip dipped in paint.

- In small groups, set all the children the task of sorting your collection of objects (see Day 5) so that all the items beginning with *h* are in the hoop labelled *h*.

Preparation

- Day 1: using Skills Master 124 or 125, write the rime *-en* and the onsets *h, m, p, t* and *th*.

- Day 5: the children will need illustrated dictionaries. You will need two hoops, a label saying *h*, and a collection of objects, most of which begin with *h*, e.g. a hammer, a hat, a toy helicopter, a horse.

DAY I

**Starter Level Big Book A pp. 39–41;
Skills Master 124 or 125**

Shared reading

- Read the action rhyme on pages 39–41 of Starter Level Big Book A to the class, pointing to the text as you do so.

- Read the rhyme a second time, looking closely at the illustrations together and performing the actions.

Focused word/sentence work

- Ask the children to help you write the word *ten* on the board, by identifying each phoneme. Choose a volunteer to write each letter.

- Ask the children to tell you how, by changing just one phoneme, you could make the word *den*. Repeat for the words *hen, men, pen* and *then*. Can anyone think of a boy's name that rhymes with *ten*? If you have a child called Ben in your class, ask him to demonstrate how to write his name on the board.

- Referring to the rhyme on pages 39–41, ask the children to find a question mark. What is the question?

- Re-read the rhyme, pausing for the class to supply the rhyming words *see, hide* and *so*.

Guided/independent work

- Give each child a word wheel or word slide using Skills Master 124 or 125 (see Preparation). Ask them to build as many words as they can using the rime *-en* and write the words they make in a list on a sheet of paper.

Plenary

- Recite the rhyme on pages 39–41, incorporating the accompanying actions you taught the class earlier. This is a rhyme that you may like to use in the future, to indicate that you would like everybody's attention before a shared activity. Alternatively, use it as a way to enable the class to move about in the middle of an activity when they have been sitting for some time or are becoming restless.

DAY 2

Starter Level Big Book A pp. 42–43; Skills Master 25

Shared reading

- Introduce the poem by Dr. Seuss on pages 42–43. How many of the children think they have read or heard something by Dr. Seuss before? Can they remember the title of the story or poem they have read or heard?
- Read the poem to the class, pointing to each word for the class to follow. Have any of the children met anyone with eleven fingers before now? Would they like to have eleven fingers? What do they think they could do with eleven fingers that they could not do with ten?

Focused word/sentence work

- Hold up your thumbs and ask the children to tell you the name of these special "fingers". Can they tell you the phoneme that the word *thumb* begins with? Write *th* on the board and challenge the class to think of words that begin with this phoneme, e.g. *than, the, then, think, thousand, three, throw*.
- Read through the second verse of the rhyme, pointing to each number in turn. Challenge children to find specific numbers within the verse, called out in random order, starting with the CVC words *six* and *ten*, before moving on to the number words with irregular spelling patterns.

Guided/independent work

- Skills Master 25 reinforces Day 2's focus on number words. As an extension activity, challenge children to find three words on the Skills Master that rhyme.

Plenary

- Re-read the rhyme by Dr. Seuss on page 43.
- Recite other counting rhymes that are familiar to your class, e.g. Once I Caught a Fish Alive or Ten Green Bottles.

DAY 3

Skills Master 26

Shared writing

- Teach the class the well-known action rhyme, If You're Happy and You Know it:

  If you're happy and you know it, clap your hands.
  If you're happy and you know it, clap your hands.
  If you're happy and you know it,
  And you really want to show it,
  If you're happy and you know it, clap your hands.

- Write the phrase *clap your hands* on the board.
- Ask the children to suggest further verses, e.g.:

  If you're happy and you know it, stamp your feet ...
  If you're happy and you know it, nod your head ...
  If you're happy and you know it, wave your hands ...

As each new verse is decided upon, list the corresponding phrase on the board underneath *clap your hands*.

- Recite the whole action rhyme again, with the children's suggested verses. Stop and point to each phrase on the board before beginning each new verse, so that the children can read the words before they begin.

Focused word/sentence work

- Write the phrase *clap your hands* on the board. Can the children find another word hidden in the word *clap*? (*lap*) Can they find three smaller words hidden in the word *hands*? (*a, an, and*)
- Ask the children to think of CVC words or non-words that rhyme with *lap*, e.g. *cap, dap, gap, map, nap, rap, sap, tap*. Give clues to CCVC words, such as *flap, snap, trap*.
- Using different onsets, build words together using the rime *-and*, e.g. *band, land, sand, stand*.

Guided/independent work

- Skills Master 26 requires children to match captions and pictures, based on ideas arising from today's shared writing activity. As an extension activity, ask children to think of another action that arose from the shared writing session. They could draw a picture demonstrating this on a separate sheet and write a caption underneath.

Plenary

- Recite the rhyme If You're Happy and You Know it once more, incorporating the children's own ideas.

DAY 4

Starter Level Big Book A p. 44; Skills Master 27

Shared reading

- Introduce the traditional rhyme *My Hands*, on page 44 of Starter Level Big Book A. Read through the rhyme slowly, pointing to the text. Re-read the rhyme together, incorporating the actions shown in the illustrations.

Focused word/sentence work

- Re-read the rhyme on page 44 with the class, pausing for them to contribute the rhyming words *face, toe, fly* and *silently*.
- Call out different parts of the body, e.g. *hands, head, shoulders, face*. See if children are able to find these in the text, drawing on critical features of words, e.g. shape, length and common spelling patterns. Can they spot the number words *one, two* and *three*?

Guided/independent work

- Skills Master 27 requires children to choose appropriate words to match the actions in the pictures.

Plenary

- Recite the rhyme on page 44, incorporating the actions. (This is another rhyme that you may like to use in the future, as a means for establishing calm when you require the children's attention.)

DAY 5

Starter Level Big Book A pp. 39–44;
Skills Masters 121–123

Shared reading

- Look briefly at each rhyme in Unit 7 and ask the children to decide which of them they would like to re-read today. Ask them to tell you what it was about their chosen rhyme that they particularly liked.

Focused word/sentence work

- Ask the children to tell you the phoneme they hear at the beginning of the word *hand*. Model the correct way to write this letter and ask the class to air trace and finger trace the shape.

- Place two hoops on the floor and label one with *h*. Using your collection of objects (see Preparation), ask the class to help you sort the objects into the correct hoops.

Guided/independent work

- Ask the children, in pairs, to draw around their partner's hand. Model the correct way to write the letter *h* and ask them to copy the letter inside their hand outline. (Alternatively, you may prefer to draw a hand shape and photocopy one for each child.)

- Using illustrated dictionaries, and referring to the items in the hoop labelled *h*, set the task of writing words beginning with *h* or drawing things that begin with *h* around their hand shape, e.g. *hamster*, *hand*, *hat*, *hen*, *hill*.

Plenary

- Using the flashcards on Skills Masters 121–123, ask the class to locate the high frequency words in the rhymes featured in Unit 7.

Consolidation and extension

- Skills Master 28 provides instructions and templates for making finger puppets. Once the children have made their puppets, teach them the following rhyme:

  Two little dicky-birds sitting on a wall;
  One named Peter and one named Paul.
  Fly away, Peter! Fly away, Paul!
  Come back, Peter! Come back, Paul!

- Teach the children actions to use with their finger puppets when reciting the rhyme: hiding the birds behind their backs to show that they have flown away and then making them reappear again at the end of the rhyme.

Unit 8 Rain or Shine

Key Learning Objectives

TL6	To re-read frequently a variety of familiar texts, e.g. big books, taped stories with texts, poems, information books
TL10	To re-read and recite rhymes with predictable and repeated patterns and experiment with similar rhyming patterns
TL11	Through shared writing: a) to understand that writing can be used for a range of purposes, e.g. to record, inform
WL1	To understand and be able to rhyme through: a) recognising, exploring and working with rhyming patterns, e.g. learning nursery rhymes b) extending these patterns by analogy, generating new and invented words in speech and spelling
WL2	Knowledge of grapheme/phoneme correspondences through: b) reading letter(s) that represent(s) the sound(s): *w* c) writing each letter in response to each sound: *w* d) identifying and writing initial and dominant phonemes in spoken words e) identifying and writing initial and final phonemes in consonant-vowel-consonant (CVC) words
WL4	To link sound and spelling patterns by: a) using knowledge of rhyme to identify families of rhyming CVC words
WL5	To read on sight a range of familiar words
WL6	To read on sight the 45 high frequency words to be taught by the end of YR
WL11	To make collections of significant words and words linked to particular topics

Range:	Traditional, nursery and modern rhymes, chant Simple non-fiction text
Texts:	*Doctor Foster*, Anon *Rain, rain, go away*, Anon From *What is the Sun?*, Reeve Lindbergh *No Rain, No Rainbow* from *Say It Again Granny*, John Agard
Resources:	Starter Level Big Book A pp. 45–49 Skills Masters 29–32 and 121–123 Listen-along Cassette Tracks 4 and 5, and Read-along Book pp. 14–16

High frequency words

a, and, away, big, can, come, day, get, go, he, I, in, is, it, like, no, of, the, to, up, you, went

Core activities

- Give each child an opportunity to revisit the traditional weather rhymes, and the non-fiction extract from *What is the Sun?* by Reeve Lindbergh, using the Listen-along Cassette (Tracks 4 and 5) and accompanying Read-along Book (pp. 14–16). Encourage them to follow the text as they listen.

- Fix a large map of the UK to the wall in the role-play area for the children to pretend to be weather forecasters. Provide them with a pointer, dressing-up clothes and accessories appropriate for all types of weather.

- In small groups, set all the children the task of sorting your collection of objects (see Day 1) so that all the items beginning with *w* are in the hoop labelled *w*.

- Ask the children to finger trace the letter shape *w* (for *weather*) in a wet sand tray.

- Help children with poor fine motor skills to make zigzag patterns, reflecting the shape of the letter w, using a variety of different art media.

Preparation

- Day 1: you will need flashcards featuring the high frequency words: *a*, *and*, *away*, *come*, *day*, *go*, *he*, *in*, *of*, *to*, *up* (see Skills Masters 121–123). You will also need two hoops, a label saying *w*, and a collection of objects, most of which begin with *w*, e.g. a wand, a watch, a whistle, wool.

- Day 4: you will need five boxes labelled with the colour words *red*, *orange*, *yellow*, *green* and *blue*. You will also need a handful of counters or cubes in each of these colours.

- Day 5: you will need different items of clothing and accessories for hot, cold and wet weather, e.g. suntan lotion, sunglasses, flip flops, woollen gloves, woollen scarf, coat, wellington boots, umbrella. You will also need three large, sticky labels with the words *hot*, *cold* and *wet* on them.

DAY 1

Starter Level Big Book A p. 45; Skills Masters 29 and 121–123

Shared reading

- Look at the main character on page 45 of Starter Level Big Book A. Who do the children think he is? What has happened to him?

- Read the nursery rhyme *Doctor Foster* on page 45. Which word rhymes with *rain*? (*again*) Re-read the rhyme, pointing at each word in turn, then find out if the children are able to spot the words *rain*, *puddle* and *middle*.

- Before you read the simple chant in the speech bubble, find out who can read the first word. Can the children find this repeated word in the nursery rhyme you have just read?

- Read the chant several times with the class, pointing to each word, then point to specific high frequency words at random and find out who can read them in isolation.

Focused word/sentence work

- Write the word *rain* on the board. Challenge the class to think of words that rhyme with *rain*, e.g. *cane*, *grain*, *mane*, *pain*, *train*. Give clues to these words if necessary. What phoneme can the children hear at the beginning of each of these words?

- Say the word *weather* and ask the class to tell you the initial phoneme. Take two hoops and label one *w*. Using your collection of objects (see Preparation), ask the class to help you sort them into the correct hoops.

Guided/independent work

- Skills Master 29 focuses on the initial phoneme *w*.

Plenary

- Recite the rhymes on page 45 of Starter Level Big Book A, both with the text and from memory.
- Using flashcards (Skills Masters 121–123), show the children high frequency words featured in the rhymes on page 45 and ask them to read them aloud. Then ask children to locate them within the text.

DAY 2

Starter Level Big Book A pp. 46–47; Skills Master 30

Shared reading

- Introduce the non-fiction extract from *What is the Sun?* by Reeve Lindbergh. Read pages 46–47. Talk about the conversational format of the text. Who do the children think the characters (narrators) are in relation to one another?
- What is the sun? Is it near or far?
- What is the rain? Do the children prefer rainy days or sunny days? Why?

Focused word/sentence work

- Slowly say the word *sun* for the children to identify the separate phonemes, then write the word on the board.
- Rub out the initial *s* and ask the class to tell you what letter you should write to make the word *bun*. Repeat for the words *fun* and *run*.

Guided/independent work

- Skills Master 30 focuses on CVC words that rhyme with *sun*. An extension activity requires children to write the answer *yes* or *no* to questions about the sun.

Plenary

- Read through the questions on Skills Master 30 together and find out whether the children answered yes or no to each question. Discuss what else the children are able to tell you about the sun and the rain.
- Are there any questions that the children would like answered about the weather? Record these questions and talk about ways in which you could find answers to these questions together, using books or computers.

DAY 3

Shared writing

- Read through the questions asked by the boy in this week's non-fiction extract. Drawing upon yesterday's plenary session, ask the children to think of questions of their own about things that puzzle or interest them about the weather. Write down some of these questions (but do not add question marks). For example:

What is snow
What are clouds made of
What are the colours of the rainbow
Where is the hottest place in the world
Where is the coldest place in the world

- Discuss how answers to the children's questions may be found, for example, in a book, on a computer encyclopaedia or the Internet, asking someone who may know, watching an information programme on television.

Focused word/sentence work

- Talk about the punctuation mark that is used at the end of a question. Does anyone know what it is called? Invite volunteers to add a question mark to each of the questions you wrote on the board. Ask the class to draw one in the air with their fingers.
- Revise CVC words that rhyme with *sun* (see Day 2).

Guided/independent work

- Ask the children to think of a question that they have about the weather. Help them to write it down and draw a question mark at the end of it.

Plenary

- Invite children to read their questions to the class. Find out if anyone in the class is able to answer them. Keep aside the unanswered questions so that you can find answers to them together at a later date, using a computer encyclopaedia or appropriate non-fiction text.

DAY 4

**Starter Level Big Book A pp. 48–49;
Skills Master 31**

Shared reading

- Look at the pictures on pages 48 and 49. What can be seen through the window on page 49? Read the title on page 48.
- Read the poem on pages 48 and 49. Does rainy weather make the children in your class frown?
- Read the second verse again, pausing for the children to read the repeated phrase "No rain, no rainbow".
- Talk about the meaning of the poem. Direct more challenging questions towards more able children. When is it possible to see a rainbow?

Focused word/sentence work

- Invite five volunteers to come to the front of the class and hold the boxes you have labelled with the colour words *red*, *orange*, *yellow*, *green* and *blue* (see Preparation). Read the words together and ask the class to tell you the initial phoneme of each word.
- Give out coloured counters to other children and invite them to come forward one at a time and put their counter in the box with the correct label. Afterwards, ask the children holding the boxes to check that all the colours match the labels. Take out any that are in the wrong box and ask the class to tell you which box they should go in.
- Explain to the class that each of the five colours you have studied can be found in the rainbow, along with

two other colours: *indigo* and *violet*. Write these words on the board for the children to see. What are the initial phonemes? Can anyone tell you what sort of colour *indigo* is? (If possible, show the class something of this colour.) Who can find three smaller words in the word *indigo* (*in, dig, go*) and at the end of the word *violet*? (*let*)

Guided/independent work

• Skills Master 31 requires children to recognise the colour words *red, orange, yellow, green, blue, indigo* and *violet*. A large rainbow is labelled with these words for the children to read and then colour each section accordingly. Remind them to begin by looking at the initial letter, which will provide a big clue to the colour word. You may like to point out the less familiar colours, *indigo* and *violet*.

Plenary

• Repeat the colour game that you played during today's focused word work session, asking different children to hold the boxes.

DAY 5

Starter Level Big Book A pp. 45 and 48–49

Shared reading

• Re-read the poem on pages 48 and 49, encouraging the class to join in where possible. Invite the children to talk about the kind of weather that they like best, inviting them to give reasons for their preferences.

Focused word/sentence work

• Ask three children to stand at the front of the class wearing large stickers with the weather words *hot, cold* and *wet* for everyone to read (see Preparation). Hand out your items of clothing and accessories one at a time to different children. Ask them to decide, with the class's help, whether they would use them in hot, cold or wet weather, then hand them over to the child with the corresponding label. The activity will be most enjoyable if the children wearing the labels put on items such as sunglasses, gloves and wellington boots, but make sure their labels can still be seen!

Guided/independent work

• Ask the children to divide a sheet of paper into two and on one side write the heading *hot* and on the other, the heading *wet*. Ask them to draw items of clothing suitable for hot and wet weather under the appropriate heading. Help them to label their items of clothing.

Plenary

• Re-read the weather rhymes on pages 45, 48 and 49.

Consolidation and extension

• Give each child a weather chart to record the weather for one week, using Skills Master 32. Read through the weather words at the bottom of the sheet and ask the children to suggest others. Find time each day during the week to complete the chart together. (You may like to repeat this exercise in a few months' time to compare winter weather words with those the children use to describe spring weather.)

• Make a collection of different weather rhymes, e.g. Incy Wincy Spider; It's Raining, It's Pouring; I hear Thunder. Print out the rhymes in a large font and display them with artwork produced by the children. Choose a different rhyme to read together each day, for as long as you have them on display.

• Make a collection of clothes and accessories appropriate for different types of weather. Categorise the clothes for a display and write labels for them together.

• Begin a display of items of different colours for the class to add to. Ask the children to help you label the different colours. Move some of the labels around when the class is not looking, then invite children to correct them.

Unit 9 Our Favourite Toys

Key Learning Objectives

TL6	To re-read frequently a variety of familiar texts, e.g. big books, taped stories with texts, poems
TL11	Through shared writing: f) to apply knowledge of the letter/sound correspondences in helping the teacher to scribe, and re-reading what the class has written
TL12	Through guided and independent writing: c) to write labels or captions for pictures and drawings
TL15	To use writing to communicate in a variety of ways, incorporating it into play and everyday classroom life
WL2	Knowledge of grapheme/phoneme correspondences through: a) hearing and identifying initial sounds in words b) reading letter(s) that represent(s) the sound(s): *a–z, ch, sh, th* c) writing each letter in response to each sound: *a–z, ch, sh, th*
WL4	To link sound and spelling patterns by: b) discriminating "onsets" from "rimes" in speech and spelling
WL5	To read on sight a range of familiar words, e.g. labels
WL6	To read on sight the 45 high frequency words to be taught by the end of YR
WL9	To recognise the critical features of words, e.g. shape, length, and common spelling patterns
WL11	To make collections of personal interest or words linked to particular topics

Range:	Poetry and stories with predictable structures Simple non-fiction text
Texts:	*New Toys, Old Toys* (illustrations) *Keith's Cupboard*, Michael Rosen
Resources:	Starter Level Big Book A pp. 50–55 Skills Masters 33–36 and 121–123 Listen-along Cassette Track 6 and Read-along Book pp. 17–20

High frequency words

a, all, and, can, day, get, go, he, in, it, like, look, mum, no, of, play, the, they, this, to, up, we, you

Core activities

- Give each child an opportunity to revisit the poem *Keith's Cupboard* by Michael Rosen, using the Listen-along Cassette (Track 6) and accompanying Read-along Book (pp. 17–20). Encourage them to follow the text as they listen to the poem.

- Set up a toy shop in the classroom for children to role-play at being shop assistants and customers. Help them to make signs (e.g. "sale", "special offer", "open", "closed"), labels and tags. Provide toy money, pretend cheques to fill out, and paper bags.

- Give each child an opportunity to make the letter *t* (for *toys*) in upper and lower case using modelling dough.

- Using magnetic letters and a paper clip on string, set up a fishing game. The task is to "catch" all the *t* letters.

- Teach the children how to play traditional games such as marbles and hopscotch. Once one group has learned how to play, ask them to explain the rules to another group.

- Using an assortment of toys for different ages, ask groups to help you sort them, for example, by deciding which toys would be suitable for babies. Ask the children to explain their reasons for selecting particular toys and rejecting others.

- Write the names of toys beginning with each letter of the alphabet on separate sheets of paper. Give one sheet to each child and ask them to draw the corresponding toy and write the initial letter in lower and upper case. The sheets may then be put together to form a class alphabet frieze. Encourage the children to help you think of a toy for each letter, using an illustrated dictionary to help with less common letters. (You may like to use words that contain, rather than begin with, less common letters, e.g. *jack-in-a-box*.)

Preparation

- Day 1: make a small collection of easily identifiable toys and write a list of their names on the board.

- Day 3: enlarge Skills Master 34 and photocopy it onto A3 paper.

- Day 4: prepare a "T tray". Collect items beginning with *t*, e.g. a teabag, a teapot, a T-shirt, a teddy, a telephone, a tie, a tin, a tomato, a toothbrush, toothpaste, a towel. Display them on a tray along with a few items that do not begin with *t*.

DAY 1

Starter Level Big Book A p. 50; Skills Master 33

Shared reading

- Turn to page 50 of Starter Level Big Book A, read the title and ask the children to identify each of the toys. Which toy would they most like to play with? Which toys would need batteries/electricity? Are the toys for children of all ages? Would all the toys be enjoyed by both boys and girls?

Focused word/sentence work

- Play I Spy using page 50. Ask the class to find a toy beginning with *t* (*teddy*), *d* (*doll*), *s* (*skateboard*), and so on.

Guided/independent work

- Skills Master 33 requires children to write the initial sound for a number of different toys.

Plenary

- See Preparation for Day 1. Ask different children to identify each of the toys in turn and then find its name on the board. They will need to be able to recognise the critical features of words: shape, length and common spelling patterns. The initial letter of each word should provide the strongest clues, but encourage the children to draw on other strategies: for example, a child looking for the word *doll* will be looking for a shorter word than *elephant*.

DAY 2

Starter Level Big Book A pp. 50–51

Shared reading

- Look briefly at page 50 again, before turning to page 51. What can the children tell you about the toys on this page? Do they have any toys like these at home? Ask the same questions as for Day 1.

Focused word/sentence work

- Play I Spy using page 51. Ask the class to find a toy beginning with *p* (*puppet*), *b* (*ball*), *m* (*monkey*), and so on.

Guided/independent work

- Ask each child to draw and label one of the old-fashioned toys that they saw on page 51.

Plenary

- Write the alphabet on the board. Ask the class to think of toys beginning with each letter. Circle each letter as you find toys that begin with that letter.

- Look again at each encircled letter. Referring to both letter names and phonemes, ask the children to recall each toy, using the initial letter as a cue.

DAY 3

Skills Master 34

Shared writing

- Enlarge Skills Master 34 and photocopy it onto A3 paper. Read through the writing frame with the class and choose a volunteer to help you fill in the spaces. Ask the child to choose a toy from your classroom so that the rest of the children can help complete the writing frame.

- Ask other children to tell you what their favourite toys are and what it is that they like best about them.

Focused word/sentence work

- Ask the class to help you write *best* on the board, identifying one phoneme at a time as you slowly say the word. Say different words that rhyme with *best* and ask the children to identify the initial phoneme, e.g. *nest*, *pest*, *rest*, *test*, *vest*, *west*. Write the onset in front of the rime -*est* to complete the new word, demonstrating the correct way to form each letter. Challenge more able children to help you write the word *chest*. Can they give you two different definitions for the word *chest*?

Guided/independent work

- Give each child a copy of Skills Master 34. Help them to complete the writing frame for themselves.

Plenary

- Refer to the shared writing session. Ask children to recall the favourite toys of particular children who shared this

information with the class. Choose different children to tell the class about the toy they like best.

- Ask the children to recall words that rhyme with *best*. Write each word on the board then read through the list together, focusing on the initial letters.

DAY 4

Starter Level Big Book A pp. 52–55

Shared reading

- Read pages 52 and 53 of the poem *Keith's Cupboard* by Michael Rosen. What do the children think about Keith? What do they think might happen next?

- Read the conclusion to the poem on pages 54–55.

- Ask the class to suggest why Keith doesn't want to play with any of his toys. Have any of the children in your class got toys that they no longer play with? What could they do with these toys?

Focused word/sentence work

- Ask the children to recall the toys in Keith's cupboard. Ask them to tell you the phoneme they hear at the beginning of each word. Write the words on the board. Ask the class to re-read them, drawing on the critical features of each word and, in particular, the initial letters.

Guided/independent work

- Present each group in turn with your "T-tray" (see Preparation). Ask the children to remove items that do not begin with *t* and write a label for the tray.

Plenary

- Choose children to read their completed writing frames and show their drawings to the rest of the class.

- Invite the rest of the children to ask questions, such as where the child likes to play with his or her toy; whether they prefer to play with it alone or with a friend; whether the toy requires batteries/electricity to work; whether the toy was new when it was given to them or was passed on from a friend or relation.

DAY 5

Starter Level Big Book A pp. 52–55; Skills Master 35

Shared reading

- Re-read the poem on pages 52–55 in its entirety, encouraging the class to join in wherever possible.

Focused word/sentence work

- Make a list of toys in the classroom, as reported to you by the children. Ask them to vote for their favourite class toy, by raising their hand, once only, as you read through the list together. Keep a tally, demonstrating how you are using writing (words and symbols) to record this information and to determine the favourite class toy.

Guided/independent work

- Skills Master 35 focuses on the initial letter *t*.

Plenary

- Make labels with the children's help to go in the toy/role-play areas of the classroom, e.g. *building bricks, toy animals, dressing-up box, home corner, farm, sand tray, toy shop*.

Consolidation and extension

- Skills Master 36 features a toy shop window. Children are required to recognise familiar names of toys, joining words to corresponding pictures in the window.

- Show the high frequency words used in the extracts to the class on flashcards using Skills Masters 121–123. Ask the children to read the words and then locate them in the poem.

- Make a collection of old and new toys. Ask children to sort them under the headings "old" and "new".

- Invite an elderly member of the community into school to talk about toys and games from their childhood.

Unit 10 Mrs Christmas

Key Learning Objectives

TL4	To notice the difference between spoken and written forms through re-telling known stories; to compare "told" versions with what the book "says"
TL12	Through guided and independent writing: b) to write their own names
TL14	To use experience of stories and simple recounts as a basis for independent writing, e.g. re-telling, and through shared composition with adults
WL2	Knowledge of grapheme/phoneme correspondences through: d) identifying and writing initial and dominant phonemes in spoken words: *c, k* e) identifying and writing initial and final phonemes in consonant-vowel-consonant (CVC) words
WL4	To link sound and spelling patterns by: a) using knowledge of rhyme to identify families of rhyming CVC words
WL5	To read on sight a range of familiar words, e.g. children's names, captions, labels, and words from favourite books
WL8	To write own name
SL4	To use a capital letter for the start of own name

Range:	Poetry and stories with predictable structures
Texts:	From *My Cat Mrs Christmas*, Adrian Mitchell *Mrs Christmas* from *All My Own Stuff*, Adrian Mitchell
Resources:	Starter Level Big Book A pp. 56–64 Skills Masters 37–40 and 121–123

High frequency words

a, all, am, and, at, big, cat, dad, day, I, in, is, it, like, mum, my, of, on, said, she, the, to, up, was, we

Core activities

- Provide the children with props to re-enact the story extract from *My Cat Mrs Christmas*. Include a soft toy cat and Christmas stockings.
- Using modelling dough, ask the children to make the letters *c* and *k*.
- Provide used Christmas cards, sheets of card and glue in the writing corner for the children to make into gift tags and Christmas cards to practise writing their own and other children's names.
- Using the hoops and collection of objects (see Day 3), ensure that everyone takes a turn at sorting the objects beginning with *c* into the correct hoop.

Preparation

- Day 2: you will need an illustrated dictionary.
- Day 3: you will need two hoops, one labelled *c*, and a collection of objects, most of which begin with *c*, e.g. *car, card, carrot, clock, comic, crisps*.

- Day 5: you will need flashcards (see Skills Masters 121–123) featuring the high frequency words contained on pages 62–64 of Starter Level Big Book A: *a, am, and, big, day, I, in, she, the, to, up, was, we*.

DAY 1

Starter Level Big Book A pp. 56–59; Skills Master 37

Shared reading

- Introduce the story extract from *My Cat Mrs Christmas* by Adrian Mitchell, which begins on page 56 of Starter Level Big Book A. Tell the class that the author of *My Cat Mrs Christmas*, Adrian Mitchell, wrote the story about his memory of one Christmas when he was a little boy.
- Read pages 56 and 57, discussing the pictures and tracking the text as you do so.
- Who is Wilfred?
- What do the class think the two boys will think of their new kitten?
- Read pages 58 and 59. Ask the class to suggest what they would have named the kitten. Ask them to show you, with their hands, how big the kitten was, given that we are told she was the size of a teacup.

Focused word/sentence work

- Ask the class to tell you the phoneme they hear at the beginning of the word *kitten*. Write this word on the board and point out the initial letter *k*. Show how this letter is formed and ask the class to finger trace the shape in the air and on a nearby surface.
- Give clues to more words beginning with *k* and write them on the board, e.g. *kangaroo, kettle, key, king, kiss, kite, koala*.

Guided/independent work

- Skills Master 37 focuses on words beginning with *k*.

Plenary

- Undertake a piece of mime with the children. Encourage each child to close their eyes and pretend that they have a parcel in their hands. Ask them to think about the shape and size of their parcel before slowly beginning to unwrap it. Tell them that you hope to be able to tell by the expressions on their faces whether or not they are pleased with what they have found inside the parcel. Once the mime is complete, ask the children to open their eyes and tell you what was inside their parcels.

DAY 2

Starter Level Big Book A pp. 56–57 and 60–61; Skills Master 38

Shared reading

- Ask the class to remind you of the story of *My Cat Mrs Christmas* so far.
- Continue to read the story extract on pages 60 and 61.
- Ask the children to tell you about all the mischievous things that Mrs Christmas got up to.

Focused word/sentence work

- Turn to page 56. Ask a child to read the title of the story extract: "My Cat Mrs Christmas".
- Ask the class to tell you the phoneme they hear at the beginning of the words *cat* and *Christmas*. Write the letter *c* on the board and point out how, in the words *cat* and *Christmas*, this letter makes the same sound as the letter *k*. Show how to write the letter *c* and ask the class to finger trace the shape in the air and on a nearby surface.
- Give clues to more words beginning with *c* and write them on the board, e.g. *camp, cap, car, carrot, cold, comic, cow, crab, crisp, cup, cut.*

Guided/independent work

- Skills Master 38 focuses on words with the initial letter *c*.

Plenary

- Using an illustrated dictionary, ask the class to predict whether there will be more words beginning with *c* or *k*. Count the number of pages for each. It may help children to know that when spelling words with an initial *k* sound, they are most likely to begin with a *c* than a *k*.
- Write the name *Mrs Christmas* on the board. Focus on the capital *C* in Christmas. Point out that the shape of the capital letter *C* is the same as the lower case letter but bigger. How many children in your class have names beginning with *C*? Ask them to write their names on the board. Underline the capital *C* in each name. Do any of these children have a name beginning with a soft *C* as in *Celine*, or *Ch* as in *Charlie* or *Charlotte*? Talk about the different phonemes that arise.
- Note how the names of Jimmy and Wilfred on pages 56 and 57 also begin with a capital letter.

DAY 3

Starter Level Big Book A pp. 56–61

Shared writing

- Invite the children to retell the story extract of *My Cat Mrs Christmas* in their own words. Compare their oral account with the printed version.
- Rewrite the story opening together in a few simple sentences.
- Encourage the class to re-read the sentences you have written together.
- See if the children are able to spot particular words that you call out within the shared writing composition. Focus on key words and high frequency words.

Focused word/sentence work

- Using two hoops, one labelled *c*, ask the class to help you sort your collection of objects (see Preparation) into the correct hoop.

Guided/independent work

- Give the children an opportunity to write a simple recount of Adrian Mitchell's childhood Christmas, using words and pictures. For many children, this will be another opportunity to practise emergent writing.

Plenary

- Re-read the entire extract from *My Cat Mrs Christmas* on pages 56–61. Pause for the class to read key parts of the story using context and picture clues, for example:

  We'll call her … (Mrs Christmas)
  Your name is … (Mrs Christmas)

DAY 4

Starter Level Big Book A pp. 62–64

Shared reading

- Read the poem by Adrian Mitchell on pages 62–64. How big did Mrs Christmas become? Compare the size she was when she grew up (*as big as your head*) with her size at the beginning of the story (*as small as a cup*).
- What details do they notice that are the same in this poem as in the story extract they have read this week?
- Can the children think of names for the new kittens? Write a few of these on the board, pointing out the capital letter at the beginning of each name.

Focused word/sentence work

- Look at the picture on page 64. Who can tell you how many kittens Mrs Christmas had? Prompt the class to help you write the word *six* on the board, by identifying the separate phonemes as you model the correct way to form each letter. What did Mrs Christmas keep her kittens in? Ask the children to help you write the word *box* on the board, underneath the word *six*. Can they spot which letter is the same?
- Show the class the correct way to form the letter *x*. Ask them to finger trace the letter *x* in the air and on a nearby surface. Give clues to other CVC words ending in *x*, e.g. *fix, fox, mix*. Slowly say each word, once the children have guessed it, and ask them to tell you the separate phonemes to help spell the word.

Guided/independent work

- Ask the children to draw Mrs Christmas's six kittens and give each one a name, making sure they use a capital letter at the start of each name.

Plenary

- Invite children to read or talk about their recount of Adrian Mitchell's childhood Christmas.

DAY 5

Starter Level Big Book A pp. 62–64; Skills Master 39

Shared reading

- Re-read the poem by Adrian Mitchell on pages 62–64.
- Ask a child to point to the title of the poem. Ask another to point to the poet's name.

Focused word/sentence work

- Read the poem once more, a verse at a time, asking the children to listen out for the words that rhyme with *cup*, *hall* and *socks*.
- Invite a child to write the word *cat* on the board. Rub out the initial letter and ask the rest of the class to

suggest other onset letters to build rhyming words and non-words using the rime -at. Write each suggestion in turn and ask the class to read it to you.

Guided/independent work

- Skills Master 39 reinforces today's work on rhyming CVC words using the rime -at.

Plenary

- Show the high frequency words used in the poem *Mrs Christmas* to the class on flashcards (see Preparation). Ask them to read the words and then locate them in the poem on pages 62–64.

Consolidation and extension

- Skills Master 40 gives children practice writing their own and other friends' names. Remind them to begin all names with a capital letter.
- Provide further opportunities for the children to practise writing their own names, for example, in Christmas cards and on gift tags.
- Read the story of *My Cat Mrs Christmas* by Adrian Mitchell in its entirety, to learn more about Mrs Christmas and her kittens.

Teacher's Notes

Starter Level
Term 2

HALF-TERMLY PLANNER

Starter Level • Term 2 • Weeks 1–5

SCHOOL _____ CLASS _____ TEACHER _____

	Phonetics, spelling and vocabulary	Grammar and punctuation	Comprehension and composition	Texts
Continuous work **Weeks 1–5**	WL 7, 10, 12, 13, 14	SL 1, 3	TL 1b, 1d, 2, 3, 11b, 11c, 11d, 11e, 12e, 13	**Range** **Fiction and poetry:** traditional, nursery and modern rhymes, chants, action verses, poetry and stories with predictable structures and patterned language **Non-fiction:** simple non-fiction texts, including recounts

Blocked work				
Week	**Unit**			**Titles**
1	11	WL 1a, 1b, 2a, 2b, 2c, 4a, 4b, 4c, 6		TL 6, 7, 10, 11f, 12d, 14	*The Grand Old Duke of York*, Traditional; *O My Grand Old Grandpa York*, Lucy Coats; *Humpty*, Grace Nichols; *Twinkle, Twinkle, Little Star*, Traditional; *Twinkle, Twinkle, Little Bat*, Lewis Carroll; *Ring-a-Ring-a-Roses*, Traditional; *Ring Around the Roses*, Stan Lee Werlin
2	12	WL 2a, 2b, 2c, 2d, 4b, 6, 9		TL 9, 11a, 12a	From *The Trouble With Grandad*, Babette Cole; *Grandad's Wonderful Marrow*, Marian Swinger
3	13	WL 2a, 2b, 2c, 2d, 2e, 6		TL 4, 5, 6, 7, 8, 9, 11f, 12d, 14	*The Enormous Turnip*, Karina Law
4	14	WL 2a, 4a, 4b, 5, 6, 8	SL 4	TL 1c, 6, 10, 12b, 12c, 14, 15	*Wet Play* from *I Hear Thunder*, David Orme (Collins *Pathways*); *Lost Property*, Karina Law; *Hometime* (illustration)
5	15	WL 1a, 2a, 2b, 2c, 2d, 4c, 6, 11		TL 6, 10, 11a, 12a, 12c, 14	*Way Down South*, Traditional American; *Monkey Tricks*, John Rice; *Lion*, Karina Law; *If You Should Meet a Crocodile*, Anon; *African Grassland*, Karina Law

TERM 2

Starter Level • Term 2 • Weeks 6–10

SCHOOL _____ **CLASS** _____ **TEACHER** _____

	Phonetics, spelling and vocabulary	Grammar and punctuation	Comprehension and composition	Texts
Continuous work **Weeks 6–10**	WL 7, 10, 12, 13, 14	SL 1, 3	TL 1b, 1d, 2, 3, 11b, 11c, 11d, 11e, 12e, 13	**Range** **Fiction and poetry:** traditional, nursery and modern rhymes, chants, action verses, poetry and stories with predictable structures and patterned language **Non-fiction:** simple non-fiction texts, including recounts

Blocked work				
Week	**Unit**			**Titles**
6	16	WL 2a, 2b, 2c, 2d, 4a, 4b, 5, 6, 9, 11		TL 1a, 6, 11a, 12a, 12c, 14	From *If You Choose me: Rabbit*, Jakki Wood; *Pets at the Vets* (illustration)
7	17	WL 1a, 2a, 2b, 2c, 2d, 3a, 3b, 3c, 4c, 6			*Apple on the Bed*, Susheila Stone (Collins *Pathways*); *Alphabet Zoo*, Karina Law
8	18	WL 1a, 2a, 2b, 2c, 2d, 2e, 6		TL 4, 6, 8, 9, 12c, 14	From *The Tusk Fairy*, Nicola Smee
9	19	WL 1a, 1b, 2a, 2b, 2c, 2d, 2e, 4c, 5, 6	SL 2	TL 6, 10, 11f, 15	*Mary had a Little Lamb*, Anon; From *Catherine and the Lion*, Clare Jarrett
10	20	WL 1a, 1b, 2a, 2b, 2c, 2d, 4c, 6, 11		TL 6, 11a, 11f, 14	*Four Seasons*, Karina Law; *Winter to Autumn* (illustration)

Focus on Literacy and the QCA Early Learning Goals

Early Learning Goals for communication, language and literacy	Unit									
	11	12	13	14	15	16	17	18	19	20
Help children to stick to the point and sensitively rephrase what they say to improve clarity and logic										
Demonstrate that the contributions of children are valued, and are used to inform and shape the direction of discussions										
Ask children to tell you about what they are going to do before they do it, and ask them to suggest possible outcomes										
Ask children to give reasons, further explanations or evidence for what they say										
Take an interest in what and how children think and not just what they know				C O N	T I N	U O U S	W	O R K		
Encourage children to explain sometimes how things work in words rather than actions										
Show interest in and build on children's own observations about letters in words										
Read children's writing so that they understand that writing is an important way of communicating										
Intervene to help children hold a pencil effectively										
Set up collaborative tasks and help children to talk and plan together about how they will begin, what parts each will play and what materials they will need	●	●	●			●		●		●
Foster children's enjoyment of spoken and written language in their play by providing interesting and stimulating opportunities	●	●			●	●		●		
Encourage children to predict possible endings to stories and events		●	●					●		
Encourage children to listen to each other and allow time for thinking, and for children to frame their ideas in words	●	●	●		●	●		●		●
Encourage children to think about the effect of the words they use	●			●	●			●	●	●
Model questions and explanations for children and help them expand on what they say						●				●
Model fluent, phrased reading with big books and encourage children to predict, take over the telling and re-tell favourite stories	●	●	●	●	●	●	●	●	●	●
Provide opportunities for talking for a wide range of purposes	●	●	●	●	●	●	●	●	●	●
Encourage children to experiment with words and sounds	●			●	●				●	
Encourage children to present and explain ideas to others and to expand on what they say				●	●	●				●
Provide opportunities for children to participate in meaningful speaking and listening activities	●	●	●	●	●	●	●	●	●	●
Encourage children to talk about how they feel				●				●	●	●
Create a story with children, asking them to predict what will happen next								●		

Early Learning Goals for communication, language and literacy	Unit									
	11	12	13	14	15	16	17	18	19	20
Help children to identify patterns, draw conclusions, explain effect, predict and speculate										●
Encourage children to explore and ask about the meanings of words		●			●	●				●
Play interactive games to encourage children to listen for the sound at the end and then in the middle of words, and use the correct letter for the sound			●							
Model writing so that children can see spelling in action and recognise how to put their knowledge of sounds to full use	●	●	●	●	●	●	●	●	●	●
Sing the alphabet							●			
Discuss different versions of the same story										
Create group poems encouraging imaginative writing such as similes	●			●	●		●		●	
Model reading while children can see the text, maintaining natural intonation and observing punctuation	●	●	●	●	●	●	●	●	●	●
Create imaginary words to describe strong characters in stories and poems					●					
Help children identify the main events in a story. Encourage the children to enact stories and to use them as the basis for further imaginative play	●		●					●		
Encourage children to add to their first-hand experience of the world through the use of books, other texts, and information and communication technology (ICT)						●	●			●
Encourage children to use a range of reading strategies by modelling different strategies and providing varied texts through which that range can be used	●	●	●	●	●	●	●	●	●	●
Write stories, poems and non-fiction texts with children	●	●	●	●	●	●	●	●	●	●
When writing, talk about what you are doing and why, and talk through some of your decision-making, such as what to write, choice of words, order. Continually re-read the writing to provide a good model for children when they write	●	●	●	●	●	●	●	●	●	●
Encourage children to use their ability to hear the sounds at various points in their writing	●	●	●	●	●	●		●	●	●
Encourage children to re-read their writing as they write	●	●	●	●	●	●	●	●	●	●
Provide materials and opportunities for children to initiate the use of writing in their play, as well as creating purposes for independent and group writing		●			●	●		●		
Give children extensive practice in writing letters, for example, labelling their work, making cards, writing notices	●	●	●	●	●	●	●	●	●	●
Continue writing practice in imaginative contexts	●	●	●	●	●	●	●	●	●	●
Use opportunities to help children form letters correctly, for example, when they label their paintings	●	●	●	●	●	●	●	●	●	●

Unit 11   Rhyming Fun

Key Learning Objectives

TL6	To re-read frequently a variety of familiar texts, e.g. big books, taped stories with texts
TL7	To use knowledge of familiar texts to re-tell to others, recounting the main points in correct sequence
TL10	To re-read and recite rhymes with predictable and repeated patterns and experiment with similar rhyming patterns
TL11	Through shared writing: f) to apply knowledge of letter/sound correspondences in helping the teacher to scribe, and re-reading what the class has written
TL12	Through guided and independent writing: d) to write sentences to match pictures or sequences of pictures
TL14	To use experience of stories, poems and simple recounts as a basis for independent writing, e.g. re-telling, substitution, extension, and through shared composition with adults
WL1	To understand and be able to rhyme through: a) recognising, exploring and working with rhyming patterns, e.g. learning nursery rhymes b) extending these patterns by analogy, generating new and invented words in speech and spelling
WL2	Knowledge of grapheme/phoneme correspondences through: a) hearing and identifying initial sounds in words b) reading letter(s) that represent(s) the sound(s): *h* c) writing each letter in response to each sound: *h*
WL4	To link sound and spelling patterns by: a) using knowledge of rhyme to identify families of rhyming CVC words b) discriminating "onsets" from "rimes" in speech and spelling c) identifying alliteration in words
WL6	To read on sight the 45 high frequency words to be taught by the end of YR

Range:	Traditional, modern and nursery rhymes
Texts:	*The Grand Old Duke of York*, Traditional *O My Grand Old Grandpa York* from *First Rhymes*, Lucy Coats *Humpty* from *No Hickory No Dickory No Dock*, Grace Nichols *Twinkle, Twinkle, Little Star*, Traditional *Twinkle, Twinkle, Little Bat*, Lewis Carroll *Ring-a-Ring-a-Roses*, Traditional *Ring Around the Roses*, Stan Lee Werlin
Resources:	Starter Level Big Book B pp. 4–8 Skills Masters 41–44, 121–123 and 124 or 125 Listen-along Cassette Tracks 7 and 8, and Read-along Book pp. 21–23

High frequency words

a, all, and, are, at, he, I, in, it, like, my, of, on, the, they, to, up, was, you

Core activities

- The Listen-along Cassette (Tracks 7 and 8) and Read-along Book (pp. 21–23) feature traditional and modern rhymes from this unit. Give each child an opportunity to use these resources to consolidate this week's reading skills and reinforce the high frequency words that appear in the text.
- Provide the children with teddy bears, a washing-up bowl to represent a bathtub, a couple of face cloths (to represent towels) and a bed for the bears, so that they can re-enact and recite the rhyme *O My Grand Old Grandpa York*.
- Toy soldiers and an improvised slope may be used to re-enact and recite *The Grand Old Duke of York*.
- Type the nursery rhyme *Humpty Dumpty* within a large, egg-shaped outline and cut it out. Cut the egg shape up into several jigsaw pieces. Ask children to put "Humpty" back together again and read the rhyme in pairs.
- Display a large wall with individual brick outlines clearly marked and a picture of Humpty sitting on it. Write high frequency words and CVC words on labels the same size as the bricks on the wall. Ask children to sort out the words, attaching those that begin with *h* to the wall.

Preparation

- Day 3: you will need an object to represent Humpty Dumpty, e.g. a hard-boiled egg with a face drawn on, or an egg-shaped pebble.

DAY 1

Starter Level Big Book B pp. 4–5; Skills Master 41

Shared reading

- Recite the rhyme on page 4 of Starter Level Big Book B with the class, pointing to each word in turn for the children to follow.
- Where did the grand old Duke of York march his men?
- Now read through the rhyme on page 5, by Lucy Coats.
- How many teds did Grand Old Grandpa York have? What did the teds do before going to bed? How did Grandpa York get the teds to sleep?

Focused word/sentence work

- Looking at page 4, ask the children to locate the high frequency word *up* (the word appears five times).
- Ask the class to identify each phoneme they hear as you slowly say the word *men* then write it on the board. Which letter would the children need to change to make the word *ten*? Can they tell you which letter you would need to change to make *ten* into *ted*? Help the class to find the words *ten* and *men* on page 4.

- Re-read the rhyme on page 5. Ask the class to find the word *teds*. Can they find a word that rhymes with *teds*? (*beds*) Ask the children to identify each phoneme they hear as you slowly say the words *ted* and *bed*, then write them on the board.
- Ask the class to find the high frequency word *and* on page 5 (the word appears three times). Now help the children to find this word hidden in the words *grand* and *grandpa*.

Guided/independent work

- Skills Master 41 requires children to cut out and sequence the different parts of the rhyme on page 5 of Starter Level Big Book B. Encourage them to re-tell the story. There is space for more able children to add a caption under each picture.

Plenary

- Re-read the rhymes on pages 4 and 5.

DAY 2

Starter Level Big Book B p. 6; Skills Master 42

Shared reading

- Recite together the traditional nursery rhyme Humpty Dumpty.
- Turn to page 6 in Starter Level Big Book B and read through the rhyme by Grace Nichols.
- Who fell off the wall? Who tried to help fix Humpty together again first? How did Hugh put Humpty together again?

Focused word/sentence work

- Ask the children to tell you the phoneme they can hear at the beginning of the names *Humpty* and *Hugh*. Who can write the letter that makes this sound on the board? Compare the shapes of capital *H* and lower case *h*. Model the correct way to draw lower case *h*, and ask the class to finger trace the shape in the air and on a nearby surface.
- Does anyone in your class have a name beginning with *H*? Invite them to write their name/s on the board. Encourage the children to think of more words beginning with *h*, e.g. *hamster, hand, hat, hedgehog, hen, hill, hippo, holiday, horse, hospital, hut.*

Guided/independent work

- Skills Master 42 provides practice in reading and writing the letter *h*.

Plenary

- Teach your class the following nonsense rhyme:

  Humpty Dumpty sat on a chair,
  Eating ripe bananas.
  Where do you think he put the skins?
  Down his new pyjamas!

  Anon

DAY 3

Starter Level Big Book B p. 6; Skills Master 43

Shared writing

- Begin by re-reading the rhyme by Grace Nichols on page 6. Tell the class that you are going to write a recount of the story of Hugh and Humpty, for the local newspaper.
- Ask the class to tell you what happened first. Help them to sequence the events of Grace Nichols' rhyme and write simple sentences to retell the story of how Humpty was fixed by Hugh and his super-glue.
- Prompt the class to help you spell high frequency words and CVC words.
- Encourage the class to help you re-read the simple recount you have written together.
- Review the recount together, checking that the details are in the correct order and asking the children if there is anything they would like to change.

Focused word/sentence work

- Say a list of words beginning with *h* and one word that does not, e.g. *hot, hit, hat, bat*. Ask the children to listen and tell you the word that does not begin with Humpty's letter.
- Sit the children in a circle and pass a hard-boiled egg or egg-shaped pebble around the circle. Ask each child to say a word beginning with *h* as they hold the "egg". Allow repeated words. Children who cannot think of a word can simply say *Humpty*.
- Think of new names for Humpty Dumpty by experimenting with the initial letters, e.g. *Rumpty Mumpty*; *Bumpty Sumpty*.

Guided/independent work

- Skills Master 43 provides a simple story board for the children to use to retell the story of Humpty and Hugh. It may be used for emergent writing practice, with the children writing a caption underneath each picture, or as a stimulus to help children in re-telling the story orally and comparing their recounts with the rhyme on page 6.

Plenary

- Re-read the poem on page 6 of Starter Level Big Book B.
- Invite children to read their story captions to the class.

DAY 4

Starter Level Big Book B p. 7; Skills Masters 124 or 125

Shared reading

- Read the traditional rhyme on page 7 before going on to read Lewis Carroll's adaptation of it.
- When and where might the children see a twinkling star? When are they most likely to see a bat? Encourage the class to think of other words to describe stars and bats.

Focused word/sentence work

- Ask the children to help you write the word *bat* on the board by identifying the separate phonemes. Encourage them to build new words by replacing the initial letter, e.g. *cat, fat, hat, mat, pat, rat, sat*. List the words that are made and ask the children to read them back to you. Build silly sentences together using some of the words, e.g. "The fat cat chased the rat."

Guided/independent work

- Using a word wheel or word slide (see Skills Master 124 or 125), investigate CVC words containing the rime *-at*.

Plenary

- Re-read the rhymes on page 7 of Starter Level Big Book B.
- Try making up new rhymes with the children based on the format of Twinkle, Twinkle, for example:

  Twinkle, twinkle, falling rain,
  I'm so sad you're here again.

  Twinkle, twinkle, little sun,
  When you shine we all have fun.

  Twinkle, twinkle, rainbow bright,
  Coloured arc of shining light.

DAY 5

Starter Level Big Book B p. 8;
Skills Masters 121–123 and 124 or 125

Shared reading

- Read the traditional rhyme on page 8. What is a pocket full of posies? (Some of the children may be interested to hear of the association of this rhyme with The Great Plague of 1665.)
- What are the children at the bottom of page 8 playing with? Read Stan Lee Werlin's adaptation of Ring-a-Ring-a-Roses. How many is a dozen?
- Divide the class into two and ask one half to read the traditional rhyme with you and the other to read Stan Lee Werlin's version. Then swap so that all the children get a turn at reading both rhymes.

Focused word/sentence work

- Using the flashcards on Skills Masters 121–123, ask the children to find the high frequency words *a, all, of, the,* and *you* in the rhymes on page 8.
- Can the children find two words that rhyme in the last line of *Ring Around the Roses*? (*get/wet*)
- Write the letter *b* on the board and ask the class to tell you the sound that it makes. Can they use it to build a word that rhymes with *wet*? Repeat, using the letters *j, l, m, n, p, s, v, y*.

Guided/independent work

- Use Skills Master 124 or 125 to investigate words with the rime *-et*.

Plenary

- Recite the rhymes on page 8 together in a circle, and think of actions to incorporate into each.

Consolidation and extension

- Skills Master 44 is a rhyming activity. Children are required to identify the pictures and join the items that rhyme. As an extension activity, ask children to try labelling some of the words. Less able children could write the initial letter next to each picture.
- Use well-known rhymes as a basis for exploring rhyming patterns though guided writing with groups of children.
- Explore nursery rhymes, such as The Grand Old Duke of York, Little Miss Muffet and Old King Cole, through role-play, re-enacting the story themes in each rhyme.

Unit 12   Grandad's Garden

Key Learning Objectives

TL9 To be aware of story structures, e.g. actions/reactions, consequences, and the ways that stories are built up and concluded

TL11 Through shared writing:
a) to understand that writing can be used for a range of purposes

TL12 Through guided and independent writing:
a) to experiment with writing in a role-play situation

WL2 Knowledge of grapheme/phoneme correspondences through:
a) hearing and identifying initial sounds in words
b) reading letter(s) that represent(s) the sound(s): *g*
c) writing each letter in response to each sound: *g*
d) identifying and writing initial and dominant phonemes in spoken words

WL4 To link sound and spelling patterns by:
b) discriminating "onsets" from "rimes" in speech and spelling

WL6 To read on sight the 45 high frequency words to be taught by the end of YR

WL9 To recognise the critical features of words.

Range:	Story with predictable structure; modern rhyme
Texts:	From *The Trouble with Grandad*, Babette Cole
	Grandad's Wonderful Marrow, Marian Swinger
Resources:	Starter Level Big Book B pp. 9–15
	Skills Masters 45–48, 121–123 and 124 or 125

High frequency words

a, all, and, at, big, for, he, I, is, it, of, said, see, the, they, to, up, was, we

Core activities

* In small groups, set all the children the task of sorting all the items beginning with *g* on your tray of objects (see Preparation) into a hoop labelled *g*.

* Give each child an opportunity to make the letter *g* in upper and lower case using modelling dough.

* Hide a selection of plastic letters, including the letter *g*, in a sand tray. Push twigs into the sand to mark the spots where a letter has been planted. Ask a small group of children to take turns "digging" under the twigs until one of them finds the letter *g*.

* Create an improvised garden area for the children to role-play digging, planting and tending seeds. Provide plastic garden tools, flower pots, a wheelbarrow and other garden paraphernalia. The area may be kept for a second week for the children to use while working on Unit 13.

* Give children the following plastic, foam or magnetic letters: *g, r, a, n, d, a, d*. Ask them to use the letters to build the word *grandad* and the smaller words within it.

Preparation

* Day 2: you will need a tray of items beginning with *g*, e.g. a game, glasses, a glove, glue, a toy goat, grapes; and some items that don't, e.g. a pencil, a sock.

DAY 1

Starter Level Big Book B pp. 9–13; Skills Master 45

Shared reading

* Introduce the extract from *The Trouble with Grandad* by Babette Cole. Read pages 9–11, up to "… growing a dangerous vegetable", to the class.

* Do any of the children's parents or grandparents grow vegetables in their gardens or allotments? Why was Grandad arrested? What do the children think will happen next?

* Read the rest of the story (pages 11–13). How did the police try to deal with the enormous tomato? What was inside it? What happened to the tomato in the end?

Focused word/sentence work

* Say the word *Grandad*. Ask the children to tell you what phoneme they hear at the beginning of the word. Write the letter *g* on the board for the children to air trace and then finger trace on a nearby surface. Watch to see that they are correctly forming the letter shape.

* How many different words can the children think of that begin with the letter *g*? (e.g. *game, garage, garden, gate, glasses, glove, glue, goal, goat, gold, good, goose, gorilla, green*) Give clues to words that the children do not think of by themselves.

Guided/independent work

* Skills Master 45 focuses on the initial letter *g*.

Plenary

* Sit the children in a circle to play an alliterative memory game called Grandad's Garden. Ask the children to repeat the sentence "I found a (something beginning with *g*, e.g. *game, glove, goat, goose, guitar*) in Grandad's garden." You may like to record the children's words on the board to be read as a list once the game is over.

* Once the children have exhausted words beginning with *g*, focus on different letters by playing, for example, Grandad's Sitting Room (words beginning with *s*).

DAY 2

Starter Level Big Book B pp. 9–13; Skills Master 46

Shared reading

* Re-read pages 9–13. Pause for the children to read key words and high frequency words by themselves.

Focused word/sentence work

* Write the word *Grandad* on the board, using large letters. How many smaller words can the class find within it? (*gran, ran, grand, a, an, and, dad*) Assist the children by covering letters to reveal the hidden words.

- How many words beginning with the letter *g* can the children remember from Day 1?

Guided/independent work

- Skills Master 46 is a reinforcement activity focusing on the initial letter *g*.

Plenary

- Present the tray of items you have collected to the class (see Preparation). Tell them that all the items should begin with the letter *g* and ask them to tell you if they can spot any that don't. These items can then be removed from the tray.

- Ask a child to write a large letter *g* on a piece of card to be displayed with the tray of objects.

DAY 3

Skills Master 47

Shared writing

- Photocopy and enlarge the writing frame on Skills Master 47 onto A3 paper. Tell the class that they are going to help you write a letter to Grandad from the police. The police are asking Grandad to stop growing such enormous vegetables as they are a danger to the public. For example:

  Dear Grandad,

  You must stop growing such enormous vegetables. They are a danger to the public. If you grow any more large vegetables, we will be forced to remove them from your allotment and you will be arrested. We suggest that you find a new hobby, such as fishing or painting.

  Signed

  P.C. Law

- The children may like to expand on a particular point, such as how Grandad's vegetables pose a threat to the community, or what will happen to Grandad if he chooses to ignore the request from the police.

Focused word/sentence work

- Re-read the letter you have composed together. Encourage the children to express opinions about what they have written and make changes if desired.

- Talk about the format of the letter. Where is the address? How does the letter begin? How does it end? Is this how the children would end a letter to a friend or relative?

Guided/independent work

- Give each child a copy of the writing frame on Skills Master 47, to develop their emergent writing skills.

Plenary

- Invite children to read or talk about their completed letters to the class. How do they think Grandad would react to such a demand? Can they think of another hobby for Grandad to take up?

DAY 4

Starter Level Big Book B pp. 9–13; Skills Masters 121–123

Shared reading

- Re-read the story extract on pages 9–13.

Focused word/sentence work

- Use the flashcards on Skills Masters 121–123 to practise reading and finding the high frequency words within the story extract.

Guided/independent work

- Ask the children to draw a picture of Grandad in his garden and write a caption about him.

- Invite children to show and talk about their pictures of Grandad.

Plenary

- Draw the children's attention to the words *big* and *bigger* on page 10. Play a boasting game. If you say, "I'm big", the class respond with "we're bigger". If you say, "I'm rich", the class respond with "we're richer", and so on.

DAY 5

Starter Level Big Book B pp. 14–15; Skills Master 124 or 125

Shared reading

- Who can identify the vegetable on page 14? Read the poem *Grandad's Wonderful Marrow* by Marian Swinger, on pages 14 and 15.

- Did Grandad's marrow win him a prize at the vegetable show? Why not?

Focused word/sentence work

- Re-read page 14. Challenge children to find the words *vegetable*, *garden*, and *win*. Write the word *win* on the board. Can the children think of any words that rhyme with *win*? (e.g. *bin, chin, din, fin, pin, tin, thin*) How many times can they see the high frequency words *big, it, was, for* and *the*?

- Turn to page 15. What does the word in the illustration say? Write the word *pop* on the board. Can the children find a word that rhymes with *pop* on page 15? Can they think of any other words and non-words that rhyme with *pop* and *stop*? (e.g. *bop, cop, hop, mop, shop, top*)

Guided/independent work

- Give each child a word wheel or word slide, using Skills Master 124 or 125. Write the rime *-op* or *-in* on the slide or wheel and add onsets for the children to practise building rhyming words. Ask the children to write the words they build on a separate sheet of paper.

Plenary

- Using the word wheels or slides (see Guided/independent work), ask the children to tell you the different words they made. Write them on the board, then read through the list together. Can any child think of any more rhyming words that could be added to the list?

Consolidation and extension

- Skills Master 48 is a sequencing activity. Children are required to cut out pictures, showing the different stages of growing a sunflower, and put them in the right order. The pictures may be stuck onto a separate sheet of paper and captions could be written underneath them during a guided writing session.

- Make a display of garden tools, seeds, plant pots, etc. Ask the children to help you identify each of the items and label them.

- Give the children an opportunity to grow something for themselves, such as a sunflower, tomato plant or cress. Record the height of the plants as they grow.

- Read *The Trouble with Grandad* by Babette Cole in its entirety, to discover what happens next.

The Enormous Turnip

Key Learning Objectives

TL4	To notice the difference between spoken and written forms through re-telling known stories; to compare "told" versions with what the book "says"
TL5	To understand how story book language works and to use some formal elements when re-telling stories, e.g. "Once there was ... "; "She lived in a little ... "; "he replied ... ".
TL6	To re-read frequently a variety of familiar texts, e.g. big books, story books, taped stories with texts
TL7	To use knowledge of familiar texts to re-enact or re-tell to others, recounting the main points in correct sequence
TL8	To locate and read significant parts of the text, speech-bubbles, italicised, enlarged words
TL9	To be aware of story structures, e.g. actions/reactions, consequences, and the ways that stories are built up and concluded
TL11	Through shared writing: f) to apply knowledge of letter/sound correspondences in helping the teacher to scribe, and re-reading what the class has written
TL12	Through guided and independent writing: d) to write sentences to match pictures or sequences of pictures
TL14	To use experience of stories as a basis for independent writing, e.g. re-telling, substitution, extension, and through shared composition with adults
WL2	Knowledge of grapheme/phoneme correspondences through: a) hearing and identifying initial sounds in words b) reading letter(s) that represent(s) the sound(s): *t* c) writing each letter in response to each sound: *t* d) identifying and writing initial and dominant phonemes in spoken words e) identifying and writing initial phonemes in consonant-vowel-consonant (CVC) words
WL6	To read on sight the 45 high frequency words to be taught by the end of YR

Range:	Story with predictable structure
Texts:	*The Enormous Turnip* retold by Karina Law
Resources:	Starter Level Big Book B pp. 16–21 Skills Masters 49–52 and 121–123 Listen-along Cassette Track 9 and Read-along Book pp. 24–29

High frequency words

a, all, and, at, cat, day, dog, for, he, in, it, of, on, said, the, they, to, up, was

Core activities

- Give every child an opportunity to re-read *The Enormous Turnip* independently using the Listen-along Cassette (Track 9) and Read-along Book (pp. 24–29).
- Cut lower and upper case t (in reverse) and T shapes onto turnip or potato halves. Give each child an opportunity to print patterns using the t and T shapes.
- Provide the children with props to re-enact the story of *The Enormous Turnip*. The improvised garden area (see Unit 12) may be used to provide a context for re-enacting the story.
- Provide a collection of vegetables, e.g. a carrot, a leek, a marrow, a potato, sprouts, a turnip, and corresponding plastic or foam initial letters. Set the task of placing each letter next to the vegetable that begins with that letter. More able children could also be asked to place the items in alphabetical order by referring to an alphabet frieze. When introducing this activity, make sure that each child is familiar with the vegetable names.

Preparation

- Days 1, 2 and 5: you will need to bring in a real turnip to show the class.
- Day 2: you will need the high frequency flashcards *dog* and *cat* (see Skills Masters 121–123), and an additional card featuring the word *mouse*.
- Day 5: draw a large outline of a turnip on an A4 sheet and photocopy one for each child. They may find illustrated dictionaries useful for the independent activity.

DAY 1

Starter Level Big Book B pp. 16–18; Skills Master 49

Shared reading

- Ask a child to point to the title on page 16 then read it to the class. How many children think they have heard this well-known story before? Talk about the pictures on pages 16 and 17.
- Read page 16. What are the opening words of the story? Talk about the phrase *Once upon a time ...*, which is often used to begin stories. Look at the way the word *enormous* has been printed. How do the children think this word should be read?
- Read page 17, then ask the children to make suggestions about what the farmer and his wife should do if they are unable to pull the turnip out of the ground.
- Read page 18. How do the children think the story will end?

Focused word/sentence work

- Ask the children to tell you the phoneme they can hear at the beginning of the word *turnip*. Invite a child to write the letter that represents this sound on the board.
- Demonstrate the correct way to write the letter *t*. Ask the children to air trace the letter, and then finger trace it on a nearby surface while you check to see that they are forming the shape correctly.

- Encourage the children to think of more words that begin with *t*, e.g. *table, tadpole, teacher, teeth, telephone, television, ten, tent, tiger, time, tortoise, toy, train, Tuesday*.

Guided/independent work

- Skills Master 49 focuses on CVC words beginning with the letter *t*.

Plenary

- Sit the children in a circle and show them a real turnip. How many have eaten turnip before? Talk about how and where turnips grow. What do they need to grow? How many children have vegetables growing in their gardens at home, or on an allotment? Do they help their parents or grandparents with jobs such as digging and watering?

- Pass the turnip around the class, asking each child to say a word that begins with *t* as they hold the turnip. If they cannot think of a word, ask them to simply say *turnip* and pass it on.

DAY 2

Starter Level Big Book B pp. 16–21; Skills Masters 50 and 121–123

Shared reading

- Re-read pages 16–18 before continuing with the story of *The Enormous Turnip*. Read to the end of the story on page 21, encouraging the class to join in with the repeated text:

  They pulled and pulled and pulled ...
  ... but the turnip was still stuck.

- Talk about how it was the tiny mouse that made all the difference in the end, and relate this to the children's own experience: when there is a job to be done, everyone's contribution is valuable.

Focused word/sentence work

- Turn to page 20. Ask the class to find the words *dog, cat* and *mouse*. Using the high frequency flashcards *dog* and *cat* (see Skills Masters 121–123), and an additional card featuring the word *mouse* (see Preparation), divide the class into three groups, assigning one animal to each. As you hold up each card in a random order, the relevant group can use a predetermined action or noise to show that they have recognised the word, e.g. a bark, mew or squeak.

- Change the groups around so that the children have a turn at identifying each animal.

Guided/independent work

- The activity on Skills Master 50 requires children to read and write high frequency words, including *cat* and *dog*.

Plenary

- Ask children to read the sentences they have completed on Skills Master 50.

- Repeat the turnip word game you played on Day 1.

DAY 3

Skills Master 51

Shared writing

- Show the class your enlarged copy of Skills Master 51. Ask them to retell the story, using the pictures.

- Decide upon a sentence or caption to be written underneath each picture.

Focused word/sentence work

- Ask the class to read back the sentences or captions you have written together.

- Call out high frequency words that appear in the sentences you have written and ask children to point these words out.

Guided/independent work

- Give each child a copy of Skills Master 51 and help them to write a caption underneath each picture to explain what is happening.

Plenary

- Ask children to read their completed storyboards to the class. Prompt the class to respond by telling the readers what they like best about their writing. Ask them to point out any differences that they notice between their friends' versions and that which they read in the Starter Level Big Book.

DAY 4

Starter Level Big Book B pp. 16–21

Shared reading

- Choose a few children to mime the story of *The Enormous Turnip* through role-play. As you re-read the text on pages 16–21, bring the children forward one at a time to play the parts of the farmer, his wife, the dog, cat and mouse. Ask the children to put their arms around the waist of the child in front of them when miming how the characters in the story tried to pull the turnip from the ground.

Focused word/sentence work

- Ask the class to help you spell some words beginning with *t*. Choose CVC words, such as *tap, ten, tin, tip, top,* and *tug*. Write the initial letter *t* each time and ask the class to listen and tell you the next two phonemes that they hear. Invite children to complete the words on the board. Ask the rest of the class to judge whether each word has been written correctly or not.

Guided/independent work

- Give children, in pairs, plastic, foam or magnetic letters or letter tiles: *a, e, g, i, n, o, p, t, u*. Ask them to make three-lettered words beginning with *t*. More able children could record the words they make.

Plenary

- Write the word *tip* on the board. Ask the children to change one letter to make the word *top*. Repeat for *ten/tin, tub/tug, tan/tap*.

DAY 5

Shared reading

- Re-read the entire story of *The Enormous Turnip* on pages 16–21. By now the children should feel confident enough to join in with most of the story. Focus particularly on the enlarged word *enormous*.

Focused word/sentence work

- Repeat the turnip word game you played on Days 1 and 2.

Guided/independent work

- Give each child a sheet with a turnip outline (see Preparation), and ask them to draw and label things that begin with *t* inside it. They may find an illustrated dictionary useful for this task.

Plenary

- Ask children to show and name the things that they have drawn inside their turnips.

Consolidation and extension

- Skills Master 52 reinforces the initial letter *t*.
- Introduce the phoneme *th* to children who are ready. Demonstrate the effect that the letter *h* has on the sound of the letter *t*. Can they think of words that begin with *th*? (e.g. *thank*, *thousand*, *thumb*, *Thursday*)
- Make a collection of different vegetables for one week. Display and label them. Talk about the way in which each vegetable grows and give the children an opportunity to paint some of them. At the end of the week, cut the vegetables so that the children can see a cross-section.
- Have a raw vegetable tasting session, using vegetables such as carrots, celery and radishes.
- Read other traditional stories with a "growing" theme, such as Jack and the Beanstalk.

Classroom Rhymes

Key Learning Objectives

TL1 Through shared reading:
c) that words can be written down to be read again for a wide range of purposes

TL6 To re-read frequently a variety of familiar texts, e.g. big books, taped stories with texts, poems, captions

TL10 To re-read and recite rhymes with predictable and repeated patterns and experiment with similar rhyming patterns

TL12 Through guided and independent writing:
b) to write their own names
c) to write labels or captions for pictures and drawings

TL14 To use experience of poems as a basis for independent writing, e.g. substitution, and through shared composition with adults

TL15 To use writing to communicate in a variety of ways, incorporating it into everyday classroom life, e.g. labels

WL2 Knowledge of grapheme/phoneme correspondences through:
a) hearing and identifying initial sounds in words

WL4 To link sound and spelling patterns by:
a) using knowledge of rhyme to identify families of rhyming CVC words
b) identifying alliteration in known and new and invented words

WL5 To read on sight a range of familiar words, e.g. children's names, captions, labels, and words from favourite books

WL6 To read on sight the 45 high frequency words to be taught by the end of YR

WL8 To read and write own name

SL4 To use a capital letter for the start of own name

Range:	Modern rhymes, chants, action verses
Texts:	*Wet Play* from *I Hear Thunder*, David Orme, Collins *Pathways* *Lost Property*, Karina Law *Hometime* (illustration)
Resources:	Starter Level Big Book B pp. 22–26 Skills Masters 53–56 and 121–123 Listen-along Cassette Track 10 and Read-along Book pp. 30–31

High frequency words

a, all, and, are, going, I, is, my, of, play, this, to, up, we

Core activities

- Give every child an opportunity to re-read *Wet Play*, by David Orme, independently using the Listen-along Cassette (Track 10) and Read-along Book (pp. 30–31).

- Provide opportunities for the children to explore different ways of writing their names, e.g. in sand, with modelling clay or with finger paints. Remind them to use a capital letter for the first letter of their names.

- Using your lost property box (See Preparation and Day 5), set children the task of sorting the collection of items so that only objects beginning with *b* are inside the box. Encourage them to find more items in the classroom beginning with *b* to go in the box.

Preparation

- Day 2: draw a simple pyramid of building bricks on A4 paper. Make each brick about 6 cm square. Photocopy one for every child. The children may find illustrated dictionaries useful for today's independent activity.

- Day 4: prepare number cards with figures (1–10) and words ("one" to "ten") for each pair of children.

- Day 5: you will need a medium-sized box and a collection of items beginning with *b*, e.g. a bag, a ball, a balloon, a banana, a bandage, a bear, a bell, a book, a boot, a brick, a brush, a toy bus, a button. You will also need a few items that do not begin with *b*.

DAY 1

Starter Level Big Book B pp. 22–23;
Skills Master 53

Shared reading

- Introduce the poem that begins on page 22. Can anyone read the title to you? Read the first two lines several times, until the children are able to recite them.

- Continue reading the poem with the children, encouraging them to join in the repeated lines.

- Discuss with the children what activities they like to do during wet play.

Focused word/sentence work

- Write the phrase *wet play* on the board. Encourage the children to discriminate the three different phonemes in the word *wet*. Challenge the children to think of words that rhyme with *wet*, e.g. *bet, get, jet, let, met, net, pet, set, yet*.

- Can anyone find a word that rhymes with *play* on page 22? Write the word *today* on the board and challenge the class to find two smaller, high frequency words within it.

Guided/independent work

- Skills Master 53 features three of the phrases based on today's rhyme: "Read a book"; "Draw and paint"; and "Build up bricks". Ask the children to draw a line matching each caption to the correct picture. There is a space for children to add another idea of their own.

Plenary

- Choose a few children to tell you the captions they wrote on Skills Master 53 and write these on the board. Take a vote to see which of the suggestions is most popular with the class. Did any of the children's phrases include a repeated initial sound? (alliteration)

DAY 2

Starter Level Big Book B pp. 22–23

Shared reading

- Re-read the rhyme on pages 22–23 with the class. Decide together on actions to go with each verse, drawing on the ideas in the pictures.
- Practise performing the rhyme together.

Focused word/sentence work

- Look at the phrases "Build with bricks" and "Sit and sulk". Emphasise the initial sounds as you read these phrases and ask the children what they notice.
- Ask the children to think of other words that begin with *b* and *s*. Make up more alliterative phrases like these.

Guided/independent work

- Give each child a sheet of A4 paper featuring building bricks (see Preparation). Ask them to draw something beginning with *b* inside each building brick. The children may find illustrated dictionaries useful for this activity.

Plenary

- Re-read the rhyme on pages 22 and 23 together, incorporating actions into the performance.

DAY 3

**Starter Level Big Book pp. 22–23;
Skills Masters 54 and 121–123**

Shared writing

- Write the following lines on the board, leaving space for a further two lines to be added:

  Wet play! Wet play!
  What are we going to do today?
  ...
  ...
  That's what I shall do!

- Ask the class to compose a line (repeated) to make a new verse for David Orme's rhyme, perhaps incorporating the ideas they used to complete Skills Master 53 on Day 1. For example:

  Drink my juice.
  Sing a song.
  Play with sand.

- With each new idea, write the child's line into the rhyme on the board and perform the new verse together. Ask the class to think of an action to go with each new idea.

Focused word/sentence work

- Using the flashcards on Skills Masters 121–123, ask the class to locate the high frequency words in the action rhyme by David Orme on pages 22 and 23: *and*, *are*, *going*, *I*, *my*, *play*, *to*, *up* and *we*.

Guided/independent work

- Skills Master 54 is a writing frame, based on today's shared writing activity, for the children to complete their own verse based on David Orme's poem.

Plenary

- Re-read the rhyme on pages 22 and 23 together, incorporating actions into the performance.
- Invite some of the children who completed their verse on Skills Master 53 to read them to the rest of the class.

DAY 4

Starter Level Big Book B pp. 24–25

Shared reading

- Introduce the second school rhyme in this unit: a counting rhyme about lost property. Begin by asking the children to tell you if they have ever lost anything. Did they eventually find what was lost? Where was it?
- Read the rhyme to the class, pointing to each number word as you read it.

Focused word/sentence work

- Ask questions such as: "How many toy animals are there?"; "How many football stickers are there?" and "How many red jumpers?" As each answer is correctly given, ask the child who supplied it to point to the corresponding number word within the poem.
- Identify the rhyming pair within each verse. (*told/mould; same/name; holes/goals; nine/mine*)

Guided/independent work

- Using the cards you have prepared (see Preparation) ask children, in pairs, to match the number words one to ten to the corresponding figures.

Plenary

- Re-read the rhyme on pages 24–25. Ask the children to tell you what word is used to describe the mitten (*stripy*), the stories (*great*), the jumpers (*red*), the hats (*woolly*), etc.

DAY 5

Starter Level Big Book B p. 26; Skills Master 55

Shared reading

- Look at the picture on page 26. Ask one of the children to point out the title of the illustration. Read the title and ask the class to talk about what they see.
- Ask the class the questions in the "To think and talk about" box.
- Talk about the use of labels in the classroom, for example, names on coat pegs.

Focused word/sentence work

- Show the children your lost property box (see Preparation). Say the word *box* and ask the class to identify the initial phoneme. Write the letter *b* on the board and ask the class to finger trace the letter shape in the air and on a nearby surface.
- Empty the contents and explain that only things beginning with *b* can go into the box. Hold up each item in turn and ask the class to tell you whether or not it can go into the box. (This game could be repeated at a later date using items beginning with different initial letters.)
- Can anyone complete the word *box* on the board?

Guided/independent work

- Skills Master 55 is a reading activity, continuing the theme of lost property.

Plenary

- Ask the children to look around the room and find examples of name labels/tags, e.g. on books, trays, clothing labels, PE bags, lunchboxes. Talk about why it is important to label your belongings in school with your name.

Consolidation and extension

- Skills Master 56 provides templates for two book plates. The children are required to write their name on each. Talk about the illustrations on each and discuss the type of book that each is appropriate for, for example, a non-fiction book and a fairy tale. Ask the children to find such books within the classroom. The book plates can be coloured and taken home to be stuck in two of the children's own books. Use this opportunity to emphasise the value of books and the importance of labelling possessions.

- Make a class book of poems based on David Orme's structure for *Wet Play*. Try other ideas such as "No school! No school! What are we going to do today?"

Unit 15   Jungle Safari

Key Learning Objectives

TL6	To re-read frequently a variety of familiar texts, e.g. big books, taped stories with texts, poems, information books, captions, own writing
TL10	To re-read and recite rhymes with predictable and repeated patterns and experiment with similar rhyming patterns
TL11	Through shared writing: a) to understand that writing can be used for a range of purposes, e.g. to record, inform
TL12	Through guided and independent writing: a) to experiment with writing in a variety of play, exploratory and role-play situations c) to write labels or captions for pictures and drawings
TL14	To use experience of poems and simple recounts as a basis for independent writing, e.g. substitution, extension, and through shared composition with adults
WL1	To understand and be able to rhyme through: a) recognising, exploring and working with rhyming patterns
WL2	Knowledge of grapheme/phoneme correspondences through: a) hearing and identifying initial sounds in words b) reading letter(s) that represent(s) the sound(s): *j, ch* c) writing each letter in response to each sound: *j, ch* d) identifying and writing initial and dominant phonemes in spoken words
WL4	To link sound and spelling patterns by: c) identifying alliteration in known and new and invented words
WL6	To read on sight the 45 high frequency words to be taught by the end of YR
WL11	To make collections of personal interest or significant words and words linked to particular topics

Range:	Story with predictable structure; modern rhyme
Texts:	*Way Down South*, Traditional American *Monkey Tricks* from *Bears Don't Like Bananas*, John Rice *Lion*, Karina Law *If You Should Meet a Crocodile*, Anon *African Grassland*, Karina Law
Resources:	Starter Level Big Book B pp. 27–33 Skills Masters 57–60 and 121–123 Listen-along Cassette Tracks 11 and 12, and Read-along Book pp. 32–34

High frequency words

a, and, are, at, big, can, cat, for, he, in, it, me, no, of, on, said, see, the, they, to, up, you

Core activities

- Turn the role-play area into a jungle for the children to play at being explorers. Suspend a simple canopy, using a hammock or net curtain, to hold toy animals from the classroom or those brought in by children. Give the children toy binoculars and notepads to make notes and draw pictures of the animals they spot. They may like to make a pretend jeep out of large cardboard boxes or chairs. Put up signs saying "Beware of the animals" and "Do not feed the animals".

- Give each child an opportunity to revisit the poems *Way Down South* and *Lion*, using the Listen-along Cassette (Tracks 11 and 12) and accompanying Read-along Book (pp. 32–34). Encourage them to follow the text as they listen to each poem.

- Give the children an opportunity to make letter *j* shapes, in upper and lower case, using modelling dough.

- Help each child to write the word *jungle* on thin card. On the reverse side, ask them to paint or draw a jungle scene. Cut the scene into several large jigsaw pieces. Ask the children to complete the jungle jigsaw; when the word *jungle* is complete, they may turn the jigsaw over to reveal the jungle scene. This activity could be repeated for other words beginning with *j*, e.g. *jumper, juggler, jar of jam, jug, jelly*.

Preparation

- Day 1: you will need a drum. Prepare a set of word cards that are large enough for the class to read. Choose mostly words that begin with *j*, e.g. *jacket, jam, jelly, jet, jigsaw, job, jog, jug, jump, jumper, jungle*. (You will need these cards again on Day 5.)

- Day 3: enlarge a copy of Skills Master 58 or copy it onto acetate for use with an overhead projector. You will also need a selection of objects (see Focused word/sentence work). If you use the examples given, these should include a hat, chocolate, a toothbrush, a plant and grapes.

- Day 4: you will need an illustrated dictionary.

DAY 1

Starter Level Big Book B pp. 27–29; Skills Master 57

Shared reading

- Read the unit title on page 27. Who can tell you what a safari is? What animals would the children expect to meet in the jungle?

- Read the traditional American rhyme on page 27. Talk about the relative sizes of elephants and grasshoppers. Where do bananas grow? Explain that it is difficult to grow bananas in the United Kingdom as it is too cold; bananas grow best in hot countries where there is plenty of sunshine, such as the Caribbean Islands.

- Introduce the poem *Monkey Tricks* by John Rice on page 28. Read the poem and ask the children to tell you which lines they heard repeated in each verse. Re-read the poem, asking the children to read the repeated lines "Deep in the jungle" and "see the Mighty Monkey".

- What do the children notice about the words *Mighty Monkey*? Ask them to think of other words beginning with *m* that could be used to describe a monkey, e.g. *Magic Monkey*, *Magnificent Monkey*, *Merry Monkey*, *Messy Monkey*, *Miserable Monkey*, *Mysterious Monkey*. Repeat for other wild animals, e.g. *tiger*, *hippo*, *crocodile*.

- Encourage the children to invent imaginary words to describe the animals.

Focused word/sentence work

- Read the unit title on page 27 again. What phoneme can the children hear at the beginning of the word? Show how to write the letter *j* on the board. Ask the children to air trace the letter, or finger trace it on a nearby surface.

- Can the children think of three months of the year that begin with *J*?

- Ask the children to stand up. Using your word cards (see Preparation), read out the words without showing them to the class. Each time the children hear you say a word that begins with the phoneme *j* they should jump up.

- Repeat the above game but this time, instead of reading the word cards, just show them to the class. The children should jump if they see a word that begins with the letter *j*. Finally, challenge children to read the words on the cards.

Guided/independent work

- Skills Master 57 focuses on words beginning with *j*.

Plenary

- Teach the class the traditional rhyme on page 27. Choose children to take turns at being the elephant; recite the first three lines with the whole class, stopping for the "elephant" to read the last line.

- Recite the poem *Monkey Tricks* on page 28 to a drum beat.

DAY 2

Starter Level Big Book B pp. 30–31; Skills Masters 121–123

Shared reading

- Using the picture clue on page 30, who can read the title of the poem? Ask the children to listen out for the rhyming words as you read the poem to the class. Read the poem a second time, encouraging the children to join in where possible and pausing for them to read the words *see* and *before*.

- Read the title *If You Should Meet a Crocodile* on page 31. Ask the children to predict what sort of advice might be given in this poem. Read the poem and ask the children to tell you the words that rhyme with *crocodile* (*smile*, *Nile*) and *thinner* (*dinner*). Explain that the Nile is a river in Africa, and point out the capital letter *N*. What do the children think might happen if they were to poke a stick at a crocodile?

Focused word/sentence work

- Using Skills Masters 121–123, show the children the following high frequency words: *a, and, big, can, cat, for, he, in, it, me, no, see, the, to, you*. Ask them to read each word in turn and then find it on page 30 or 31 of Starter Level Big Book B.

Guided/independent work

- Provide a selection of illustrated dictionaries, word books and appropriate non-fiction books. Set a research task: ask the children to look for pictures of animals that they might find in the jungle. Give them Post-it Notes or something similar so that they can mark the relevant pages. Look through these together at an appropriate time.

Plenary

- Test the children's ability to read the high frequency words located on pages 30 and 31 of Starter Level Big Book B once more (see Focused word/sentence work).

- Re-read the poems on pages 30 and 31.

DAY 3

Skills Master 58

Shared writing

- Enlarge a copy of Skills Master 58 or copy it onto acetate for use with an overhead projector. Tell the class that they are going to help you write a jungle poem that will be similar in style to *Monkey Tricks* by John Rice. The first line of each verse will be the same: "Deep in the jungle".

- Read through the writing frame together and ask the children to think of alliterative phrases (an animal and a word that describes it) to write into the spaces, e.g. "crafty crocodile"; "lazy lion"; "hungry hippo". Each time a suggestion is made that everyone likes, write it into the space and read through the new verse together.

Focused word/sentence work

- Begin an alliterative sentence, e.g. "The hungry hunter lost his ... ". Hold up two items, one of which begins with the same initial phoneme as most of the words in the sentence, e.g. *hat*. Ask the children to tell you which object you should choose to complete the sentence. Other sentences you might like to use are:

  A cheeky chimpanzee stole my (*chocolate*).
  The tiger tried to eat my (*toothbrush*).
  A pretty pink parrot pecked my (*plant*).
  A greedy gorilla grabbed my (*grapes*).

Guided/independent work

- Skills Master 58 is a writing frame that provides children with an opportunity to complete their own jungle poems. Encourage them to think about different ideas, in groups, before deciding what they would like to write. Help them to write the words they have chosen to fill in the spaces, then listen to them as they read their completed poems.

Plenary

- Invite children to read their completed poems to the rest of the class.

DAY 4

Shared reading

- Introduce the non-fiction text on pages 32 and 33. See if the children are able to identify each of the animals. Read the text and talk about the information that is given. Which of these animals do children like best and why?

Focused word/sentence work

- Ask a child to find and point to the word *chimpanzee*. What phoneme can the children hear at the beginning of this word? Write the word on the board and underline the initial phoneme.

- Ask the class to look and listen for two other words containing *ch* as you re-read page 32 (*reach, munch*).

- Ask the class to think of other words that begin with the *ch* phoneme. Write these on the board. Look up words beginning with *ch* in an illustrated dictionary to see if there are any other words that the children have not thought of.

Guided/independent work

- Skills Master 59 focuses on the *ch* phoneme.

Plenary

- Create opportunities for the children to explore the *ch* phoneme. Ask them to chatter like chimpanzees: "chatter, chatter, chatter"; munch like giraffes: "munch, munch, munch"; crunch like crocodiles: "crunch, crunch, crunch"; chirp like a tropical bird: "chirp, chirp, chirp"; call for the cheetahs: "cheetah! cheetah! cheetah!" Think of actions to go with each sound.

DAY 5

Shared reading

- Re-read the information text on pages 32 and 33. Ask the questions in the "To think and talk about" box.

Focused word/sentence work

- Revise the letter *j* by playing the game you played on Day 1. Ask the children to stand up. Using your word cards (see Preparation), read out the words without showing them to the class. Each time the children hear you say a word that begins with the phoneme *j* they should jump up.

- Repeat the above game but this time, instead of reading the word cards, just show them to the class. The children should jump if they see a word that begins with the letter *j*. Finally, challenge children to read the words on the cards.

Guided/independent work

- Ask the children to choose their favourite jungle animal, draw a picture of it and label it. Help them to write a non-fiction caption or sentence about it.

Plenary

- Invite children to show their pictures and read their sentences and captions about jungle animals.

- Ask the children to vote for their favourite poem from Unit 15. Learn and recite the chosen poem.

Consolidation and extension

- Skills Master 60 reinforces high frequency colour words. Children have to follow a code, using initial letters, in order to colour a jungle scene.

- Make a class collage of a jungle scene with lots of lush, green foliage. Include the elephant, lion and crocodile from the poems in Unit 15. Copy and display the corresponding poems alongside them. Add the Mighty Monkey, from John Rice's poem, swinging on the vines. Label her *hairy knees*, *coconut nose* and *dancing feet*.

- Make a class anthology of Jungle Poems. Include the poems written by the children, using Skills Master 58.

Unit 16   Pets and Vets

Key Learning Objectives

TL1	Through shared reading: a) to recognise printed and handwritten words in a variety of settings, e.g. labels, forms, lists
TL6	To re-read frequently a variety of familiar texts, e.g. big books, information books, own and other children's writing
TL11	Through shared writing: a) to understand that writing can be used for a range of purposes, e.g. to record, inform
TL12	Through guided and independent writing: a) to experiment with writing in a variety of play, exploratory and role-play situations c) to write labels or captions for pictures and drawings
TL14	To use experience of simple recounts as a basis for independent writing
WL2	Knowledge of grapheme/phoneme correspondences through: a) hearing and identifying initial sounds in words b) reading letter(s) that represent(s) the sound(s): *r, v* c) writing each letter in response to each sound: *r, v* d) identifying and writing initial and dominant phonemes in spoken words
WL4	To link sound and spelling patterns by: a) using knowledge of rhyme to identify families of rhyming CVC words b) discriminating "onsets" from "rimes" in speech and spelling
WL5	To read on sight a range of familiar words, e.g. captions, labels
WL6	To read on sight the 45 high frequency words to be taught by the end of YR
WL9	To recognise the critical features of words, e.g. shape, length, and common spelling patterns
WL11	To make collections of personal interest or significant words and words linked to particular topics

Range:	Simple non-fiction text
Texts:	From *If You Choose Me: Rabbit*, Jakki Wood *Pets at the Vet's* (illustration)
Resources:	Starter Level Big Book B pp. 34–40 Skills Masters 61–64 and 124 or 125

High frequency words

a, and, at, away, can, day, for, get, go, I, in, is, it, like, of, on, me, my, the, this, to, up, you

Core activities

- Make a collection of soft toy animals for the children to role-play at being vets. Encourage the children to incorporate writing into their role-play by filling in simple forms for each animal that is brought into the "surgery". Ask them to write the pet's name, the type of animal that it is, the age of the pet, and the problem. Encourage the children to give each other advice about how they should look after their pets.

- Give each child an opportunity to make the letters *r* and *v* using modelling dough or finger paints.

- Provide a selection of non-fiction books about animals for the children to look at. Give them specific tasks, such as finding information and pictures about rabbits.

Preparation

- Day 1: you will need magnetic letters and a metal tray or board (or something similar) to spell the word *rabbit*.

- Day 3: ask the children to bring in photographs of their own pets. If they do not have any pets, they may bring in a toy animal. You will need a picture of a pet or a soft toy animal of your own; alternatively you may refer to a class pet or toy.

DAY 1

Starter Level Big Book B pp. 34–37; Skills Master 61

Shared reading

- Introduce the non-fiction text that begins on page 34 from *If You Choose Me: Rabbit*. Find out how many children own a rabbit and ask them to tell you whatever they know about looking after their pet.

- Read through the information on pages 34–35 with the class. Pause before selected words, e.g. *hutch, nest, hot*, encouraging the children to supply them by drawing on context clues, illustrations and focusing on initial sounds. Refer back to the information given by children who own a rabbit, as appropriate.

- Talk about the pictures on pages 36–37. See if the children are able to identify each item before reading the labels to them.

- When might a rabbit owner need to use a carrying box? What would the brush and comb be used for? Why would the food bowl need to be heavy? What is sawdust? Explain what a mineral lick is for. Why should the hay that a rabbit eats be kept in a hay rack?

- Discuss the purpose of the log for keeping a rabbit's teeth from getting too long. Do the children know of any other animals whose teeth continue to grow? (e.g. a hamster) Reassure the children that a rabbit does not feel pain when gnawing, or having its teeth trimmed by a vet.

Focused word/sentence work

- Write the word *rabbit* on the board. Without reading the word, ask the children to tell you the sound that the initial letter represents. Can they think of a colour beginning with *r*? Does anyone's name begin with *r*? (Write any children's names on the board and compare the different shapes of the capital and lower case letters.) Can the children find anything else in the room that begins with this sound?

- Encourage the class to think of other words beginning with *r*, e.g. *radio*, *railway*, *rainbow*, *rat*, *read*.

Guided/independent work

- Skills Master 61 focuses on the initial letter *r*.

Plenary

- Using magnetic letters on a metal tray or board, spell the word *rabbit*. Which letter appears twice in the word?

- Cover the first four letters in the word *rabbit* and ask the class to read the smaller word *it*. Cover the first three letters to reveal the word *bit*. Then cover the last three letters and ask them to read the non-word that remains.

- Challenge the class to see how many different words they can make using the letters in the word *rabbit*. Invite children to come forward and spell some of the words they think of, using the magnetic letters, while you write the words on the board, modelling the correct way to form each letter as you do so. Some possibilities the children may think of are: *a*, *i* (point out that a capital *I* is needed for this word), *at*, *bat*, *bib*, *bit*, *it*, *rib* and *tab*.

DAY 2

Starter Level Big Book B pp. 36–39; Skills Master 62

Shared reading

- Ask the children to read each of the labels on pages 36–37 to you.

- Read the remaining section of this extract on pages 38 and 39 to the class. Discuss information that is new to the children and ask the questions in the "To think and talk about" box.

Focused word/sentence work

- Close the Starter Level Big Book and slowly say the word *rabbit*. Ask the children to help you spell the word on the board, by identifying each phoneme. See who can remember that there are two letter *b*s in the word.

- Ask the children to help you make a list of the things that a rabbit needs. Write each item as it is suggested to form a list.

Guided/independent work

- Skills Master 62 requires each child to think about the things a rabbit needs. Explain that they should put a tick next to the things a rabbit needs and a cross next to those that it does not need.

- More able children who complete this task within the given time could try writing the initial sound of each item beside it.

Plenary

- Find out from the class which of the items on Skills Master 62 they think a rabbit needs.

- Play I Spy using the objects on Skills Master 62.

DAY 3

Starter Level Big Book B pp. 36–37

Shared writing

- Present your picture of a pet or soft toy animal to the class (see Preparation). Tell the class that they are going to help you write about your pet.

- Write the name of your pet and the type of animal it is. Write about the type of home it needs, taking advice from the class. Ask the children to suggest the sort of things your pet would like to eat, and make a list. Write about any other needs your pet has, such as regular exercise or something to gnaw on.

Focused word/sentence work

- Encourage the class to re-read your shared writing. Encourage them to pick out particular words that you call out, such as key words, CVC words or high frequency words. Is there anything that they would like you to add or change?

Guided/independent work

- Ask the children to draw a picture of their pet (see Preparation) and write about its needs. They may like to draw and label the things that their pet needs; leave Starter Level Big Book B open at pages 36 and 37 to remind the children of how this was done in the extract from *If You Choose Me: Rabbit*. Children who have not brought in a picture or soft toy may like to write about the pet that you focused on during the shared writing session, or a soft toy animal belonging to the classroom. Alternatively, they may focus on the rabbit that they have studied in this week's non-fiction extract.

Plenary

- Give children the opportunity to read each other's writing about their pets and show their pictures. Prompt the children to ask their partners questions about the pet they have written about.

DAY 4

Starter Level Big Book B p. 40; Skills Master 124 or 125

Shared reading

- Introduce the scene depicted on page 40. Can the children tell you what the picture is showing?

- Ask the class the questions in the "To think and talk about" box. What else can the children see in the picture?

- Discuss with the class the sort of things that a vet might want to know if you were to visit him or her with a sick pet.

Focused word/sentence work

- Play I Spy using the scene on page 40.
- Write the words *pet* and *vet* on the board. What do the children notice about these two words? Explore different onsets with the rime -*et*, to make non-words and words, e.g. *get, jet, let, met, net, set, wet, yet*.

Guided/independent work

- Give each child a word wheel or word slide, using Skills Master 124 or 125. Write the rime -*et* and add onsets for the children to build words. Ask them to write the words they make on a separate sheet.

Plenary

- Ask the children to tell you the different words they made using the word wheels or slides (see Guided/ independent work). Ask them to help you write the words on the board by segmenting the separate phonemes, and think of more words to add to the list of rhyming words.

DAY 5

Starter Level Big Book B p. 40; Skills Master 63

Shared reading

- Briefly revisit the scene depicted on page 40.
- Engage in a role-play situation, with a confident child playing the part of a vet. Present your "pet" to them. Give them a chance to ask you appropriate questions. Tell them the problem, for example: "My rabbit isn't eating his food. I leave lots of delicious cakes and sweets in his hutch but he just ignores them" or "Her teeth are too long." Encourage the child, with suggestions from the class, to offer you advice, such as suggesting the correct types of food for a rabbit, or asking if your rabbit has a log in his hutch to chew on.

Focused word/sentence work

- Write the word *vet* on the board. Ask the children to tell you the phoneme they hear at the start of the word *vet*.
- Write the letter *v* on the board for the children to air trace and finger trace. Check to see that they are forming the letter correctly.
- Ask the children to think of words beginning with *v*, e.g. *van, vegetable, velvet, video, village, violin, volcano*. Give clues to some of these words if necessary.

Guided/independent work

- Skills Master 63 focuses on CVC words ending in the rime -*et*.

Plenary

- Explore a few more role-play situations with the class, focusing on different types of pets. Draw on the knowledge of children who have these pets at home.

Consolidation and extension

- Skills Master 64 focuses on words beginning with *v*.
- Display photographs and drawings of the children's own pets and toy animals, along with labels and captions about them.
- Bring a real rabbit into the class. Invite the owner to talk about their pet and answer questions from the children.

Unit 17   A to Z

Key Learning Objectives

WL1   To understand and be able to rhyme through
     a) recognising, exploring and working with
     rhyming patterns

WL2   Knowledge of grapheme/phoneme
     correspondences through:
     a) hearing and identifying initial sounds in words
     b) reading letter(s) that represent(s) the sound(s):
     a–z, ch, sh, th
     c) writing each letter in response to each sound:
     a–z, ch, sh, th
     d) identifying and writing initial and dominant
     phonemes in spoken words

WL3   Alphabetic and phonic knowledge through:
     a) sounding and naming each letter of the
     alphabet in lower and upper case
     b) writing letters in response to letter names
     c) understanding alphabetical order through
     alphabet books, rhymes, and songs

WL4   To link sound and spelling patterns by:
     c) identifying alliteration in known and new and
     invented words

WL6   To read on sight the 45 high frequency words to
     be taught by the end of YR

Range:	Story with predictable structure; modern rhyme
Texts:	*Apple on the Bed*, Susheila Stone, Collins *Pathways* *Alphabet Zoo*, Karina Law
Resources:	Starter Level Big Book B pp. 41–47 Skills Masters 65–68 Listen-along Cassette Track 13 and Read-along Book pp. 35–38

High frequency words

a, and, away, cat, dad, in, me, my, of, on, the, to, up

Core activities

- Give every child an opportunity to re-read *Alphabet Zoo* independently using the Listen-along Cassette (Track 13) and Read-along Book (pp. 35–38).

- Provide a collection of alphabet books for the children to read and refer to.

- Hang a low, string washing line across the room and attach 26 pegs. Collect pictures of items beginning with each letter of the alphabet, or photocopy pictures from alphabet books, and give the children opportunities in small groups to peg the pictures to the washing line in the correct order. Move some of the pictures from time to time and see who can spot which pictures are in the wrong places.

- Provide children with a complete set of lower case letters and a handful of upper case letters, using plastic, foam or magnetic letters or word cards. Ask them to find the lower case letters that correspond with each upper case letter.

Preparation

- Display an alphabet frieze at a height that is easily accessible to the children. You will need a set of foam or plastic letters, letter tiles or cards throughout this unit.

- Days 2, 3 and 4: children may need illustrated dictionaries for the independent activities.

- Day 5: you will need a set of foam or plastic upper case letters, or upper case letter tiles or cards.

DAY 1

Starter Level Big Book B pp. 41–43; Skills Master 65

Shared reading

- Begin by reciting the alphabet with the class or singing an alphabet song.

- Talk about the pictures on pages 41–43.

- Encourage the children to read along with you, following the text, as you read *Apple on the Bed* by Susheila Stone.

Focused word/sentence work

- Point out how there is a word beginning with every letter of the alphabet in the text you have just read. Recite the alphabet with the children, pointing to the initial letter of each of these words to prove this.

- Using an alphabet frieze as a reference point, ask the children to tell you what letter comes after *d* and so on, calling out letters randomly. Then ask the children to tell you what letter comes before *s* and so on.

Guided/independent work

- Skills Master 65 is a join-the-dots activity. The dots are labelled with the letters of the alphabet. By joining these in sequence, the children will reveal a picture.

Plenary

- Hand out a letter of the alphabet to each child. Call out letters randomly. As each child hears his or her letter being called, they run to the alphabet frieze and touch the corresponding letter. After a while, ask children to swap letters with a friend and play the game again. This game reinforces letter positions in the alphabet sequence.

DAY 2

Starter Level Big Book B pp. 41–43

Shared reading

- Encourage the class to re-read *Apple on the Bed* on pages 41–43 with little help from you. Divide them into two groups and challenge each group to read alternate lines. The children should easily be able to read the words using the picture cues. This text provides an opportunity for children to practise reading the high frequency words *a, in, on* and *the*.

Focused word/sentence work

- Using the text *Apple on the Bed* on pages 41–43, ask the class to tell you which word starts with the letter *g* and so on, using letter names rather than sounds.
- Compare the different shapes of the upper and lower case letters on pages 41–43. Which of the capital letters do the children think look the same only slightly larger? (e.g. *C, O, P, S, V, W, X, Z*)

Guided/independent work

- Explain to the class that they are going to help make an alphabet frieze like the one you have displayed. Give each child a sheet of A4 paper and a letter of the alphabet. Ask them to write their letter (in upper and lower case) on the sheet of paper and draw something that starts with that letter. Children may find an illustrated dictionary useful for completing this activity.

Plenary

- Call out each letter of the alphabet in turn and ask the children with the corresponding letter to come forward and hold up their picture. Check that all their letters are correctly formed in both upper and lower case. Arrange the children, in alphabetical order, standing in a circle so that they may see each other's work. If there are more than 26 children in your class, ask children with the same letters to stand together.
- In alphabetical order, ask each child, in turn, to call out his or her letter and hold up their picture.
- The children's pictures may be displayed together to form an alphabet frieze.

DAY 3

Skills Master 66

Shared writing

- Ask the class to help you make an alphabet poem. Start the poem in this way, using words that the children suggest:

  a is for apple
  b is for bed
  c is for cat

  Continue with this task for as many letters of the alphabet as possible in the time that you have.

Focused word/sentence work

- Call out different words that the children used in the shared writing activity. Ask the children to tell you which letter starts each word that you say.
- Sing or recite the alphabet together.

Guided/independent work

- Skills Master 66 reinforces today's shared writing activity. Once children have completed the activity, they may continue working through the alphabet, starting with *h*, on a separate sheet using the same format (*h is for ...*). Encourage them to see how many letters they can work through, using an illustrated dictionary for ideas. Challenge more able children to complete each sentence with a word rather than a picture, as you did during the shared writing session.

Plenary

- Stand in a circle. Practise passing a ball or bean bag to a child who then returns it to you. Repeat this several times and then tell the children that you are going to try to recite the alphabet together. Each time a child catches the ball, they must say aloud the next letter of the alphabet. As the ball is passed back to you each time, the whole class repeats the letter.

DAY 4

Starter Level Big Book B pp. 44–47

Shared reading

- Read the poem on pages 44–47. Are the children able to tell you why this poem is called *Alphabet Zoo*?
- How would they feel if their home were invaded by animals?

Focused word/sentence work

- Read the first line of the poem on page 44. Which words start with *a*? Which words in the second line begin with *b*? Working your way through the poem, see how many words the children are able to find for different letters of the alphabet.
- Talk about letters that don't make their usual sound, e.g. *o* in *opened* and *u* in *used* and *unicorn*. Explain that while we expect *o* to sound like *o* in *octopus* and *u* to sound like *u* in *umbrella*, the children will sometimes hear these letters sounding like their letter names in words.

Guided/independent work

- Give children pictures or objects to arrange in alphabetical order in pairs.

Plenary

- Re-read the poem *Alphabet Zoo* on pages 44–47.

DAY 5

Starter Level Big Book B pp. 44–47; Skills Master 67

Shared reading

- Re-read the poem *Alphabet Zoo* on pages 44–47, encouraging the children to join in, particularly with the last word of each line.

Focused word/sentence work

- Challenge children to identify key words in the poem *Alphabet Zoo*, e.g. *ant, bed, shed, egg, frog, pen, den, fox, zoo*.
- Write the word *zoo* on the board. Ask the children to make the sound that they hear at the beginning of this word. Can they find another word on page 47 that begins with the letter *z*? (*zebra*) Give them clues to other words that begin with *z*, e.g. *zigzag, zip*, and the name *Zoe*.

Guided/independent work

- Skills Master 67 is a reinforcement activity focusing on the initial letter *z*.

Plenary

- Hand out an upper case letter to each child (see Preparation). Call out the letters randomly. As each child hears his or her letter being called, they should run to the alphabet frieze and touch the corresponding letter. After a while, ask children to swap letters with a friend and play the game again.

Consolidation and extension

- Skills Master 68 requires children to match upper and lower case letters.
- Make a class alphabet book using the format established in the shared writing session on Day 3.

Unit 18   The Tusk Fairy

Key Learning Objectives

TL4	To notice the difference between spoken and written forms through re-telling known stories; to compare "told" versions with what the book "says"
TL6	To re-read frequently a variety of familiar texts, e.g. big books, story books, poems, own writing
TL8	To locate and read significant parts of the text, e.g. speech-bubbles, italicised, enlarged words
TL9	To be aware of story structures, e.g. actions/reactions, consequences, and the ways that stories are built up and concluded
TL12	Through guided and independent writing: c) to write sentences to match pictures or sequences of pictures
TL14	To use experience of stories as a basis for independent writing, e.g. re-telling, substitution, extension, and through shared composition with adults
WL1	To understand and be able to rhyme through: a) recognising, exploring and working with rhyming patterns, e.g. learning nursery rhymes
WL2	Knowledge of grapheme/phoneme correspondences through: a) hearing and identifying initial sounds in words b) reading letter(s) that represent(s) the sound(s): *e* c) writing each letter in response to each sound: *e* d) identifying and writing initial and dominant phonemes in spoken words e) identifying and writing initial and final phonemes in consonant-vowel-consonant (CVC) words
WL6	To read on sight the 45 high frequency words to be taught by the end of YR

Range:	Story with predictable structure
Texts:	From *The Tusk Fairy*, Nicola Smee
Resources:	Starter Level Big Book B pp. 48–53 Skills Masters 69–72 and 121–123

High frequency words

a, all, and, day, for, it, look, of, on, said, see, she, the, they, to, up, was, you

Core activities

- Set up a toy hospital within the classroom for role-play. Explain that this is a place where toys who, like Lizzie's elephant, have "been through a lot" and are looking "rather the worse for wear" may be brought to be cared for.
- Make up a bed for Lizzie and her toy elephant with a pillow underneath which the children can leave messages for the Tusk Fairy.

- Provide a selection of objects that begin with the short *e* sound as in *egg, elephant, engine, envelope* (not as in *earrings* or *Easter*) along with other objects that do not. Ask the children to sort them into two hoops, one of which is labelled *e*. Alternatively, provide pictures of objects beginning with this *e* sound along with pictures of objects that do not; ask the children to sort out the pictures of things beginning with the short *e* sound and put them into a large envelope marked *e*.
- Give each child an opportunity to make the letter shape *e*, in upper and lower case, using modelling dough or finger paints.
- Provide the children with props to re-enact the story of *The Tusk Fairy*.

Preparation

- Day 3: enlarge a copy of Skills Master 70 or copy it onto acetate for use with an overhead projector.

DAY 1

Starter Level Big Book B pp. 48–50; Skills Master 69

Shared reading

- Ask a child to point to the title on page 48. Read the title and ask the children to tell you what they think a tusk fairy might be. Ask someone to point to the elephant's tusks in the picture.
- Read page 48. Have any of the children in your class got a knitted animal? How old do they think Lizzie and the elephant are?
- Read pages 49 and 50 and talk about the pictures. Ask the class to describe how Lizzie must be feeling.

Focused word/sentence work

- Close the book and ask the children to listen carefully as you say the word *elephant*. What phoneme do they hear at the beginning of the word? Write the letter *e* on the board for the class to air trace and finger trace.
- Explain that not many words begin with this phoneme, but that the sound can be heard in the middle of lots of words. Give clues to CVC words containing *e*, e.g. "you sleep in one of these" (*bed*); "the number after nine" (*ten*); "a colour" (*red*); "a chicken that lays eggs is called this" (*hen*); "the opposite of no" (*yes*). Ask the children to help you write the words on the board, by identifying the separate phonemes as you slowly say each word.

Guided/independent work

- Skills Master 69 focuses on CVC words containing *e*.

Plenary

- Remind the children that there are not many words beginning with the short vowel *e* and then challenge them to think of some, e.g. *egg, elbow, eleven, empty, end, engine, enjoy, envelope, exit, explain, explore*. Give clues to help them think of some of these words if necessary.

DAY 2

Starter Level Big Book B pp. 48–53

Shared reading

- Re-read pages 48–50, encouraging the children to join in with high frequency words and with phrases and sentences they remember.
- Read page 51. What do the class think will happen if Lizzie puts the tusks under her pillow?
- Read the end of the story extract on pages 52 and 53.

Focused word/sentence work

- Can the children find a word on page 49 that is printed in capital letters? Why is the word *TERRIBLE* printed in upper case letters? Ask the children to re-read this sentence, placing extra emphasis on the word *TERRIBLE*.
- Turn to page 53. Can the children read you the sentences that have been written in capital letters? Ask them to explain why these words are in upper case letters and to tell you how they should be read.

Guided/independent work

- Lizzie thinks that the Tusk Fairy has made Elephant better. Ask the children to draw a picture of what they think the Tusk Fairy looks like. During a guided writing group session, help the children to add a caption to their drawings.

Plenary

- Invite children to show and talk about their pictures of the Tusk Fairy.

DAY 3

Skills Master 70

Shared writing

- Using an enlarged copy of Skills Master 70, encourage the children to tell the story of a broken toy using the pictures. What happens in the beginning? In the middle? At the end?
- Ask the children to help you compose sentences to tell the story.

Focused word/sentence work

- Encourage the children to re-read the sentences they composed with you. Focus on key words and high frequency words.

Guided/independent work

- Give each child a copy of Skills Master 70 and help them to tell the story about a broken toy using the pictures.

Plenary

- Encourage the children to re-read the sentences they composed with you on the enlarged copy of Skills Master 70. Cut out the four sections. Attach them to the board in the wrong order. Re-read the sentences together and challenge the children to help you put them back in the right sequence.
- Invite children to read their stories to the rest of the class.

DAY 4

Starter Level Big Book B pp. 48–53;
Skills Masters 121–123

Shared reading

- Re-read the story extract on pages 48–53, encouraging the children to join in with high frequency words, and with phrases and sentences they remember.

Focused word/sentence work

- Using the flashcards on Skills Masters 121–123, challenge the class to read the following high frequency words and find them in the text on pages 48–49 of Starter Level Big Book B: *a, and, day, for, look, on, she, the, they, to, was*.

Guided/independent work

- Provide materials for the children to make a thank you card for the Tusk Fairy from Lizzie.

Plenary

- Invite children to show and talk about the cards they have made for the Tusk Fairy. Encourage them to read any messages they have added.

DAY 5

Starter Level Big Book B pp. 48–53;
Skills Masters 71 and 121–123

Shared reading

- Ask the class to re-tell the story of the Tusk Fairy.
- Re-read the story extract on pages 48–53. Pause for children to supply high frequency words, and key phrases and sentences.
- Compare the children's re-telling of the story with what the book says.

Focused word/sentence work

- Using the flashcards on Skills Masters 121–123, challenge the class to read the following high frequency words and find them in the text on pages 50–53: *all, it, of, said, see, up, you*.

Guided/independent work

- The activity on Skills Master 71 provides practice in developing observational skills and pencil control.

Plenary

- Teach the children to recite the rhyme *An Elephant*:

  An elephant goes like this and that,
  He's terribly big,
  And he's terribly fat.
  He has no fingers,
  And he has no toes,
  But goodness gracious,
  What a long nose!

  Traditional

  Encourage the class to help you think of actions to go with the rhyme.

Consolidation and extension

- Skills Master 72 features the rhyme *An Elephant* for the children to read and complete. Once the children have learned the rhyme, they could take the Skills Master home and practise reading it to their families.

- During a guided group writing session, help the children compose a thank you letter from Lizzie to the Tusk Fairy.

- Read the book, *The Tusk Fairy*, by Nicola Smee, to the class in its entirety.

Unit 19　School Visitors

Key Learning Objectives

TL6　To re-read frequently a variety of familiar texts, e.g. big books, story books, taped stories with texts, poems, own writing

TL10　To re-read and recite rhymes with predictable and repeated patterns and experiment with similar rhyming patterns

TL11　Through shared writing:
f) to apply knowledge of letter/sound correspondences in helping the teacher to scribe, and re-reading what the class has written

TL15　To use writing to communicate in a variety of ways, incorporating it into play and everyday classroom life, e.g. recounting their own experiences

WL1　To understand and be able to rhyme through:
a) recognising, exploring and working with rhyming patterns, e.g. learning nursery rhymes
b) extending these patterns by analogy, generating new and invented words in speech and spelling

WL2　Knowledge of grapheme/phoneme correspondences through:
a) hearing and identifying initial sounds in words
b) reading letter(s) that represent(s) the sound(s): *l*
c) writing each letter in response to each sound: *l*
d) identifying and writing initial and dominant phonemes in spoken words
e) identifying and writing initial and final phonemes in consonant-vowel-consonant (CVC) words

WL4　To link sound and spelling patterns by:
c) identifying alliteration in known and new and invented words

WL5　To read on sight a range of familiar words, e.g. children's names, and words from favourite books

WL6　To read on sight the 45 high frequency words to be taught by the end of YR

SL2　To use awareness of the grammar of a sentence to predict words during shared reading and when re-reading familiar stories

Range:	Nursery rhyme; story with predictable structure
Texts:	*Mary had a Little Lamb*, Anon From *Catherine and the Lion*, Clare Jarrett, Collins
Resources:	Starter Level Big Book B pp. 54–59 Skills Masters 73–76 Listen-along Cassette Track 14 and Read-along Book pp. 39–43

High frequency words

a, all, and, at, big, come, day, for, get, go, he, I, in, it, like, me, of, on, play, said, see, she, the, they, to, up, was, went, yes, you

Core activities

- Give every child an opportunity to re-read the extract from *Catherine and the Lion* independently, using the Listen-along Cassette (Track 14) and Read-along Book (pp. 39–43).

- Introduce a toy animal into the classroom, ideally a lion or a lamb, for the children to include and incorporate into their work and play. Ask the children to think about what the "new class member" might need to know, such as where coats and bags belong, what happens at break-time and lunchtime, how to sit and listen while the class register is taken, etc. (Children may be reminded of the way in which they looked after Lion or Lamb, and how they included him or her in their games, when new children join the class.)

- Give each child an opportunity to make the letter shape *l*, in upper and lower case, using modelling dough or finger paints.

- Provide a selection of objects that begin with *l*, e.g. a leaf, a lemon, a lollipop, a lorry, along with other objects that do not. Ask the children to sort them into two hoops, one of which is labelled *l*.

Preparation

- Day 1: you will need Post-it Notes (cut to size) or something similar, to cover the word *Mary* on page 54 of Starter Level Big Book B.

- Days 2 and 5: you will need a toy lamb or lion.

- Day 5: draw a lion template on A4 paper and photocopy one for each child. You will also need a crown; if you cannot find one among the children's dressing up items, a child could be asked to make a simple crown using a strip of card (like the one Catherine made for Lion on page 59 of Starter Level Big Book B). Children will need illustrated dictionaries for the independent activity.

DAY 1

Starter Level Big Book B p. 54; Skills Master 73

Shared reading

- Read the first verse of the nursery rhyme on page 54, pointing at the words for the children to follow as they join in with reciting the rhyme. How many of them already know it?

- How many children know the second verse of this rhyme? Read through the second verse together. What do the class think Mary's teacher will have to say about the lamb following her to school? What do they think the headteacher would say if one of them brought a lamb to school? What sort of trouble do they think the lamb might cause?

- Teach the children the whole rhyme so that they are able to recite it.

Focused word/sentence work

- Read the rhyme on page 54 again and ask the children to tell you the words that rhyme with *snow*, *rule* and *day*.

- What sound can the children hear at the beginning of the words *little* and *lamb*?

- Cover the word *Mary*, which appears twice in the first verse, with Post-it Notes or something similar. Invite a child to come forward and write their name on them (if you have a mixed class, invite a girl). Re-read the rhyme with the new name in place. Replace the Post-it Notes and ask another child to come forward and write their name on them. (Invite a boy to come forward the second time, if you have a mixed class.) As you re-read the two verses, the children should point out that the second verse does not make sense. Ask them to explain how to resolve the problem (by replacing *her* with *his*). Draw the children's attention to the capital letter at the start of each name.

Guided/independent work

- Skills Master 73 focuses on the first verse of the nursery rhyme *Mary had a little lamb*. Encourage children to follow the words as they recite the rhyme. Ask them to suggest what the teacher in the picture might be saying. Help them to write the words they suggest in the speech bubbles.

Plenary

- Re-read the nursery rhyme on page 54.
- Make up rhymes using the same rhyming structure for the children to complete, for example:

      Mary had a little mouse,
      Its fur was soft and white.
      The mouse would sleep all through the day,
      And play all through the ... (*night*).

      Mary had a little cat,
      It wasn't very nice.
      It liked to scare the birds away
      And chase away the ... (*mice*).

DAY 2

Starter Level Big Book B pp. 55–56; Skills Master 74

Shared reading

- Ask a child to point to the title on page 55. Read the first word of the title and challenge the class to read the remaining words for you.
- Read page 55, drawing on the clues given by the illustrations. Ask the children what they would think if they woke up and found a lion in their bedroom. What would they want to ask or tell him?
- Read page 56. Ask the children to tell you what they need to remember to bring to school each day. Do they think Lion will enjoy going to school?

Focused word/sentence work

- Write the word *lion* on the board. Ask the class to say the sound that they hear at the beginning of the word. Model the correct way to write the letter *l* and ask the children to air trace the shape or finger trace it on a nearby surface. Can they think of another animal that begins with *l*? (Remind them of Day 1's nursery rhyme, if necessary.)

- Sit the children in a circle and ask them to think of words beginning with *l*. Pass a toy lamb or lion to the nearest child with his or her hand in the air. Once a child is holding the toy, they may say the word they are thinking of, before passing it on to the next child with their hand in the air.

Guided/independent work

- Skills Master 74 focuses on words beginning with *l*.

Plenary

- Discuss how the children in your class felt on their first day at school. Did they feel excited or frightened or both? What were they afraid of? What did they look forward to? What did they enjoy most about their first day?

DAY 3

Skills Master 75

Shared writing

- Explain to the class that it might be quite frightening for a lion to go to school for the first time. Ask them to tell you the sort of things that he might be afraid of. For example, he might be afraid of all the children. He might be afraid that they would think he was stupid if he didn't know the answer to a question the teacher asked. He might be afraid of getting lost in such an enormous building, etc.
- Tell the children that Lion might not be so afraid if he knew a little about what to expect. Ask them to help you write about what they do at school.
- Begin with the words "At school we ...".

Focused word/sentence work

- Ask the class to help you make up silly sentences using words that begin with *l*. For example:

      Lazy lions like to lie on sun loungers.
      A leaping lizard leapt onto my lap.
      Leo likes to lick lemon lollies.
      Ladybirds look before they leap.

Guided/independent work

- Skills Master 75 provides spaces for children to write about, and illustrate, two aspects of school life. A sentence opener is provided to help them get started: "At school we ...".

Plenary

- Invite children, in pairs, to read each other's sentences and look at their pictures.

DAY 4

Starter Level Big Book B pp. 57–59

Shared reading

- Continue reading the story of *Catherine and the Lion* on pages 57–59.
- Ask the questions in the "To think and talk about" box.

Focused word/sentence work

- Look again at the last paragraph on page 59. What did Catherine give Lion?
- Write the word *big* on the board and ask the class to read it. Challenge a child to change the word into *bug* by changing just one letter. Challenge another child to change *bug* into *hug* by changing one more letter. Continue in this way, building the words *hut, hit, sit, sat, bat, bag* and *big*. Point out that this was the word you started with.

Guided/independent work

- Give children, in pairs, plastic, foam or magnetic letters or letter tiles: *a, b, g, h, i, t, u*. Ask them to make three-lettered words. More able children could record the words they make.

Plenary

- Repeat the word chain activity (See Focused word/sentence work) with the children's help.

DAY 5

Starter Level Big Book B pp. 55–59

Shared reading

- Re-read the entire extract from *Catherine and the Lion* on pages 55–59. Encourage the children to tell you what they like best about the story.

Focused word/sentence work

- Repeat the game that you played on Day 2: sit the children in a circle and ask them to think of words beginning with *l*. Pass a toy lamb or lion to the nearest child with his or her hand in the air. Once a child is holding the toy, they may say the word they are thinking of, before passing it on to the next child with their hand in the air.

Guided/independent work

- Using illustrated dictionaries, set the children the task of finding words beginning with *l*. They may enjoy writing the words, or drawing the objects, on a lion template (see Preparation).

Plenary

- Ask a volunteer to come forward and pretend to be Lion. Give them a chair to sit on and a crown to make them feel the part. Invite the rest of the class to ask Lion questions about his first day at school: Did he feel afraid? What did he do at breaktime? What did he do after lunch? Did he like going to school?

Consolidation and extension

- Skills Master 76 presents word chains, similar to the one you explored with the class on Day 4. The children need to change one letter at a time to build new CVC words.
- Read the story of *Catherine and the Lion* by Clare Jarrett in its entirety.
- During a guided writing session, help the children to make a timetable of a typical day in your class.

Unit 20 | The Changing Year

Key Learning Objectives

TL6	To re-read frequently a variety of familiar texts, e.g. big books, information books, captions, own writing
TL11	Through shared writing: a) to understand that writing can be used for a range of purposes, e.g. to record, inform f) to apply knowledge of letter/sound correspondences in helping the teacher to scribe, and re-reading what the class has written
TL14	To use experience of simple recounts as a basis for independent writing
WL1	To understand and be able to rhyme through: a) recognising, exploring and working with rhyming patterns b) extending these patterns by analogy, generating new and invented words in speech and spelling
WL2	Knowledge of grapheme/phoneme correspondences through: a) hearing and identifying initial sounds in words b) reading letter(s) that represent(s) the sound(s): *s, w, y* c) writing each letter in response to each sound: *s, w, y* d) identifying and writing initial and dominant phonemes in spoken words
WL4	To link sound and spelling patterns by: c) identifying alliteration in known and new and invented words
WL6	To read on sight the 45 high frequency words to be taught by the end of YR
WL11	To make collections of words linked to particular topics.

Range:	Simple non-fiction text
Texts:	*Four Seasons*, Karina Law *Winter to Autumn* (illustration)
Resources:	Starter Level Big Book B pp. 60–64 Skills Masters 32, 77–80 and 124 or 125

High frequency words

a, and, are, day, for, in, is, it, like, look, of, on, the, they, this, to, you

Core activities

- Make a collection of dressing-up clothes for different seasons, e.g. hats, scarves, gloves, coats, umbrellas, swimming costumes/trunks, sandals, Wellington boots, shorts, sun glasses, jumpers. Ask the children to sort them into two boxes, labelled "summer" and "winter". Encourage them to explain their decisions.
- Give each child an opportunity to make the letter *y* using modelling dough, or to finger paint it using yellow paint.
- Fix a large map of the United Kingdom to the wall in the role-play area for the children to pretend to be weather forecasters. Provide them with a pointer and dressing up clothes appropriate for different times of the year.
- Give children another opportunity to sort the items in your mystery bag (see Day 3) into two hoops labelled *s* and *w*.

Preparation

- Day 2: you will need a pebble, or an item associated with summer, such as a sun hat, sunglasses or a bottle of sun lotion.
- Day 3: prepare plain cards for each child to write a letter on each side. You will also need a bag full of mystery items beginning with *s*, e.g. scissors, a toy snake, soap, a sock, a toy spider, string, sweets, and *w*, e.g. a wand, a watch, a whistle, wool. You may like to include a few distracters that begin with neither letter.
- Day 4: you will need an illustrated dictionary.
- Day 5: make a collection of dressing-up clothes for different seasons, e.g. hats, scarves, gloves, coats, umbrellas, swimming costumes/trunks, sandals, Wellington boots, shorts, sun glasses, jumpers. Try to provide enough items of clothing for every child.

DAY 1

Starter Level Big Book B pp. 60–61; Skills Master 77

Shared reading

- Read the unit title and the subheading *Winter*. Explain that winter is a season. How many seasons are there in each year? Who can tell you the names of each of the other three seasons? Which season do the children think it is now?
- What do the children know about winter? Read page 60 together, encouraging the children to join in with high frequency words and words for which there are strong context clues. How many children have helped to build a snowman before? What sort of clothes keep them warm in winter? Can the children tell you the names of any animals that sleep throughout the winter months?
- Who can tell you which season comes after winter? Read page 61.

Focused word/sentence work

- Point to the unit title on page 60 once again and ask the class to read it to you. What sound can they hear at the beginning of the word *Year*?
- Model the correct way to write the letter *y* on the board for the children to air trace and finger trace on a nearby surface.
- Using an alphabet frieze, show the children where the letter y comes in the alphabet. Open an illustrated dictionary at the letter *y*, pointing out that it comes towards the end of the dictionary. How many words can the children see that begin with *y*? Read them together.
- Explain that, although there are not many words that begin with *y* the children will find the letter in lots of words, e.g. *my, by, cry, dry, fly, fry*. Write a few examples on the board for the children to read.

Guided/independent work

- Skills Master 77 focuses on words that contain the letter *y*.

Plenary

- Read the last paragraph on page 61 again, asking the children to listen out for a word beginning with *y*.

- Say a number of words to the class and ask them to repeat them, replacing the initial letter each time with the phoneme *y*. Begin with words the children will recognise, e.g. *mess* (*yes*); *shell* (*yell*). Move on to build nonsense words, e.g. *rip* (*yip*); *jog* (*yog*).

DAY 2

**Starter Level Big Book B pp. 62–63;
Skills Master 124 or 125**

Shared reading

- Ask the children to remind you of the seasons they read about on pages 60–61. Which season comes next? Ask them to read the title on page 62 before reading the text. What sort of clothes keep the children cool in summer?

- Ask the class to read the title on page 63. You may like mention the fact that *a* at the beginning of *autumn* is not making its usual sound. What phoneme can the children hear at the beginning of *autumn*? Explain simply that the sound of *a* sometimes changes if, for example, it is followed by the letter *u*. More able children may also spot that there is a redundant letter *n* at the end of the word.

- What can the children tell you about autumn? Talk about hibernation. Do the children know what the word means? Can they tell you the names of any animals that hibernate in winter? Which animals can they see in the pictures?

Focused word/sentence work

- Play a rhyming game called Hot Sun. Ask the children to help you identify the separate phonemes and write each word on the board. Sit the children in a circle and pass your pebble or other object (see Preparation) around the circle. As each child takes hold of the pebble, he or she should say a word that rhymes with *hot*. Accept nonsense words that rhyme and repeated words. If a child gets stuck, they may simply repeat the word *hot* and pass the pebble on. Repeat for the word *sun*.

Guided/independent work

- Using a word wheel or word slide (see Skills Master 124 or 125), ask each child to investigate the rime *-ot* using the onsets *c, d, g, h, j, l, p* or *r*. Ask the children to write the words they make, or spell them on a table top using foam or plastic letters.

Plenary

- Write a selection of season-related words on the board, e.g. *sun, rain, snow, Christmas, fireworks, birthday, flowers, green, brown, butterflies, bees, ice-cream, coat, mittens*. Read through the words a couple of times and then pause at each one, asking the children which season or seasons the word makes them think of.

DAY 3

Skills Master 78

Shared writing

- Ask the children to tell you their favourite season. Choose one of the seasons to write about (it would be a good idea to choose the current season so that the children can draw upon the present experience).

- Complete the sentence, "My favourite season is ... " on the board. Ask the children to tell you what they like most about the chosen season. Find different ways to complete the sentence, "I like it because ... ", drawing on as many different ideas as possible.

- Discuss how the reasons for liking a particular season will vary for different children. One child may like winter best because that is when they celebrate Christmas; another may like winter because they like playing in the snow.

Focused word/sentence work

- Hand out cards to the children and ask them to write a *w* on one side for *winter*, and an *s* on the other side for *summer*.

- Take your bag of mystery objects (see Preparation) and hold them up one at a time for the class to see. Ask the children to hold up their card to show *w* or *s*, depending on the initial sound of the object you are holding.

Guided/independent work

- Skills Master 78 provides a simple writing frame for children to begin writing about their favourite season. Have the names of each of the four seasons displayed clearly somewhere, for the children to copy.

Plenary

- Invite children to read their completed sentences to the rest of the class.

DAY 4

Starter Level Big Book B pp. 60–63; Skills Master 79

Shared reading

- Re-read pages 60–63.

Focused word/sentence work

- Write the words *summer* and *winter* on the board, side by side. Divide the class into two groups, assigning one word to each group. Alternate between the two groups, asking the first to find more words that begin with *s* and the second to find words beginning with *w*. List the words you are given under the corresponding season. Read through the lists together.

- Using an illustrated dictionary, show children that there are many more words beginning with *s* than with *w*. Was this reflected in the word game you just played?

Guided/independent work

- Skills Master 79 features a chart showing the four seasons. Underneath are pictures for the children to cut out and stick in the season that they consider to be the most appropriate. Encourage the children to discuss their decisions before sticking the pictures down.

Plenary

- Hold a seasons quiz to develop speaking and listening skills. Ask the children questions relating to the seasons. For example, "Which season comes after summer?"; "Which season comes after spring?"; "During which season is it most likely to snow?"; "During which season is Christmas celebrated?"; "During which season is Halloween?"

DAY 5

Starter Level Big Book B p. 64

Shared reading

- Open Big Book B at page 64. Can any of the children read the title to you? Ask them to tell you what they see on page 64. Can they explain the illustrated chart? What are the children in the pictures doing? Encourage the class to point out as many of the different features of each season as possible. Talk about the cyclic nature of the seasons and the way that this is reflected in the illustrations.

Focused word/sentence work

- Give each child an item of clothing (see Preparation). Ask them to hold up their item when you call out the sound of the initial phoneme. Ask the whole class to repeat each phoneme.

Guided/independent work

- Give each child a sheet of paper with the heading *summer* or *winter*. Ask them to draw a picture of themselves wearing clothes suitable for the season identified on their sheet. Help them to label parts of their drawings, e.g. *hat, coat, boots*.

Plenary

- Invite children to read the title on their sheet, show the class their drawing and explain what items of clothing they are wearing in the picture and why.
- Make up alliterative sentences together, focusing on the letter *s* for *season, spring* and *summer*. Talk about how you like to spend a summer day, for example:

  I like to sit in the sun on a summer day.
  I like to splash about in the sea on a summer day.
  I like to suck sugary sweets on a summer day.
  I like to sing silly songs on a summer day.

Consolidation and extension

- Skills Master 80 focuses on CVC words beginning with *s*.
- Make a class frieze showing the seasons of the year. Include a tree to show the changes that occur at different stages of the year. Add words that the children associate with each season to the display, e.g. winter: *cold, frost, hibernate, ice, snow*; spring: *blossom, buds, green, rain, sun*; summer: *flowers, holiday, hot, sun, warm*; autumn: *brown, bulbs, fog, gold, leaves, mist, rain, wind*.
- Using Skills Master 32, observe and record a week's weather during spring. Compare the results with those recorded during Unit 8.
- Revisit the weather rhymes learned during Unit 8. Discuss which season each rhyme reflects. Make a class anthology of seasonal/weather rhymes.

Teacher's Notes

Starter Level
Term 3

TERM 3

Starter Level • Term 3 • Weeks 1–5

SCHOOL _____   CLASS _____   TEACHER _____

	Phonetics, spelling and vocabulary	Grammar and punctuation	Comprehension and composition	Texts
Continuous work **Weeks 1–5**	WL 7, 10, 12, 13, 14	SL 1, 3	TL 1b, 1d, 2, 3, 11b, 11c, 11d, 11e, 12e, 13	**Range** **Fiction and poetry:** traditional, nursery and modern rhymes, chants, action verses, poetry and stories with predictable structures and patterned language **Non-fiction:** simple non-fiction texts, including recounts

Blocked work				
Week	**Unit**			**Titles**
1	21	WL 2a, 2b, 2c, 2e, 6	SL 2	TL 5, 6, 10, 11f, 14	From *A Dark, Dark Tale*, Ruth Brown
2	22	WL 2a, 2b, 2c, 2d, 4a, 4b, 4c, 5, 6, 11	SL 4	TL 1a, 6, 11a, 12a, 12b, 15	*People at Work*, Karina Law; *In the Street* (illustration)
3	23	WL 2a, 2b, 2c, 2e, 4c, 6	SL 2	TL 4, 6, 11f, 15	From *The Baked Bean Queen*, Rose Impey; *It's Time for Lunch Rosie!*, Tony Bradman
4	24	WL 2a, 2b, 2c, 2d, 2e, 3a, 3c, 6		TL 6, 9, 11a, 11f, 12a	From *Alexander and the Dragon*, Katharine Holabird; *Our Dragon*, Wendy Larmont
5	25	WL 1a, 1b, 2e, 4a, 4b, 6, 11	SL 2	TL 6, 11a, 11f	*Night Sounds*, Berlie Doherty; From *Big Fat Hen and the Red Rooster*, Vivian French; *Early Country Morning*, Grace Nichols

TERM 3

Starter Level • Term 3 • Weeks 6–10

SCHOOL _____ CLASS _____ TEACHER _____

	Phonetics, spelling and vocabulary	Grammar and punctuation	Comprehension and composition	Texts
Continuous work **Weeks 6–10**	WL 7, 10, 12, 13, 14	SL 1, 3	TL 1b, 1d, 2, 3, 11b, 11c, 11d, 11e, 12e, 13	**Range** **Fiction and poetry:** traditional, nursery and modern rhymes, chants, action verses, poetry and stories with predictable structures and patterned language **Non-fiction:** simple non-fiction texts, including recounts

Blocked work				
Week	**Unit**			**Titles**
6	26	WL 2a, 2b, 2c, 2d, 3a, 3b, 3c, 5, 8, 11	SL 4	TL 1a, 12b, 15	*The Yummy Alphabet*, Chris Lutrario (Collins *Pathways*)
7	27	WL 2a, 2b, 2c, 2d, 2e, 3a, 3b, 3c, 4c, 5		TL 1c	From *My ABC Dictionary* (Collins)
8	28	WL 2a, 2b, 2c, 2d, 2e, 4a, 4b, 6	SL 2	TL 4, 5, 6, 7, 8, 9, 11f, 12d, 14	*The Gingerbread Man*, Karina Law
9	29	WL 2a, 2b, 2c, 2d, 6, 9, 11	SL 2	TL 6, 10	*Algy Met a Bear*, Anon; *All About Bears*, Karina Law; *Here a Bear, There a Bear*, John Foster
10	30	WL 1a, 1b, 2a, 2b, 2c, 2d, 2e, 4a, 4c, 5, 6		TL 7, 9, 10, 14	From *Where's Tim's Ted?*, Ian Whybrow and Russell Ayto

TERM 3

Focus on Literacy and the QCA Early Learning Goals

Early Learning Goals for communication, language and literacy	Unit									
	21	22	23	24	25	26	27	28	29	30
Help children to stick to the point and sensitively rephrase what they say to improve clarity and logic										
Demonstrate that the contributions of children are valued, and are used to inform and shape the direction of discussions										
Ask children to tell you about what they are going to do before they do it, and ask them to suggest possible outcomes										
Ask children to give reasons, further explanations or evidence for what they say										
Take an interest in what and how children think and not just what they know				CONTINUOUS WORK						
Encourage children to explain sometimes how things work in words rather than actions										
Show interest in and build on children's own observations about letters in words										
Read children's writing so that they understand that writing is an important way of communicating										
Intervene to help children hold a pencil effectively										
Set up collaborative tasks and help children to talk and plan together about how they will begin, what parts each will play and what materials they will need		●	●	●	●	●		●		●
Foster children's enjoyment of spoken and written language in their play by providing interesting and stimulating opportunities	●	●	●	●	●	●		●		●
Encourage children to predict possible endings to stories and events	●			●				●		●
Encourage children to listen to each other and allow time for thinking, and for children to frame their ideas in words	●	●		●				●		●
Encourage children to think about the effect of the words they use	●			●						
Model questions and explanations for children and help them expand on what they say		●		●						
Model fluent, phrased reading with big books and encourage children to predict, take over the telling and re-tell favourite stories	●	●	●	●	●	●	●	●	●	●
Provide opportunities for talking for a wide range of purposes	●	●	●	●	●	●	●	●	●	●
Encourage children to experiment with words and sounds, for example, in nonsense rhymes	●				●		●			
Encourage children to present and explain ideas to others and to expand on what they say into, for example, complete statements or questions		●		●					●	
Provide opportunities for children to participate in meaningful speaking and listening activities	●	●	●	●	●	●	●	●	●	●
Encourage children to talk about how they feel										
Create a story with children, asking them to predict what will happen next	●									

Focus on Literacy Starter Level Teacher's Resource Book © HarperCollins*Publishers* Ltd 2001

Early Learning Goals for communication, language and literacy	Unit									
	21	22	23	24	25	26	27	28	29	30
Help children to identify patterns, draw conclusions, explain effect, predict and speculate										
Encourage children to explore and ask about the meanings of words	●						●			
Play interactive games to encourage children to listen for the sound at the end and then in the middle of words, and use the correct letter for the sound		●	●	●	●			●		
Model writing so that children can see spelling in action. Encourage children to apply their own knowledge of sounds to what they write	●	●	●	●	●	●	●	●	●	●
Sing the alphabet				●		●	●			
Discuss different versions of the same story								●		
Create group poems encouraging imaginative writing	●								●	
Model reading while children can see the text, maintaining natural intonation and observing punctuation	●	●	●	●	●	●	●	●	●	●
Create imaginary words to describe strong characters in stories and poems				●						
Help children identify the main events in a story. Encourage the children to enact stories and to use them as the basis for further imaginative play			●	●	●			●		●
Encourage children to add to their first-hand experience of the world through the use of books, other texts, and information and communication technology (ICT)		●					●		●	
Encourage children to use a range of reading strategies by modelling different strategies and providing varied texts through which that range can be used	●	●	●	●	●	●	●	●	●	●
Write stories, poems and non-fiction texts with children	●							●	●	
When writing, talk about what you are doing and why, and talk through some of your decision-making, such as what to write, choice of words, order. Continually re-read the writing to provide a good model for children when they write	●	●	●	●	●	●	●	●	●	●
Encourage children to use their ability to hear the sounds at various points in their writing	●	●	●	●	●	●	●	●	●	●
Encourage children to re-read their writing as they write	●	●	●	●	●	●	●	●	●	●
Provide materials and opportunities for children to initiate the use of writing in their play, as well as creating purposes for independent and group writing		●		●		●				●
Give children extensive practice in writing letters, for example, labelling their work, making cards, writing notices	●	●	●	●	●	●	●	●	●	●
Continue writing practice in imaginative contexts	●	●	●	●	●	●	●	●	●	●
Use opportunities to help children form letters correctly, for example, when they label their paintings	●		●	●		●	●	●	●	●

Unit 21 — A Dark, Dark Tale

Key Learning Objectives

TL5	To understand how story book language works and to use some formal elements when re-telling stories
TL6	To re-read frequently a variety of familiar texts, e.g. big books, story books, taped stories with texts, poems, wall stories
TL10	To re-read and recite stories with predictable and repeated patterns and experiment with similar patterns
TL11	Through shared writing: f) to apply knowledge of letter/sound correspondences in helping the teacher to scribe, and re-reading what the class has written
TL14	To use experience of stories as a basis for independent writing
WL2	Knowledge of grapheme/phoneme correspondences through: a) hearing and identifying initial sounds in words b) reading letter(s) that represent(s) the sound(s): *m, o, x* c) writing each letter in response to each sound: *m, o, x* e) identifying and writing initial and final phonemes in consonant-vowel-consonant (CVC) words
WL6	To read on sight the 45 high frequency words to be taught by the end of YR
SL2	To use awareness of the grammar of a sentence to predict words during shared reading and when re-reading familiar stories

Range:	Story with predictable structure and patterned language
Texts:	From *A Dark, Dark Tale*, Ruth Brown
Resources:	Starter Level Big Book C pp. 4–7 Skills Masters 81–84 Listen-along Cassette Track 15 and Read-along Book pp. 44–47

High frequency words

a, and, at, in, of, on, the, up, was

Core activities

- Ask each child to re-read *A Dark, Dark Tale* by Ruth Brown, using the Listen-along Cassette (Track 15) and Read-along Book (pp. 44–47).

- Using the items from Day 2 (see Preparation), give every child an opportunity, in pairs or small groups, to sort out the items beginning with the letter *m* and put them in the box labelled *m*.

- Provide modelling dough for the children to make the letters *o* and *x*.

- Having taught the children how to play Noughts and Crosses, provide nine square grids and the letters *o* and *x* for them to play the game in pairs. (Refer to the letters *o* and *x* rather than noughts and crosses.)

Preparation

- Day 2: you will need a large box containing items beginning with *m*, e.g. a magazine, a magnet, a map, marmalade, a mask, a toy mouse, a milk carton, a mirror, a toy monkey, a mug. Include a few items that do not begin with *m*.

  Draw a large outline of a mouse on A4 paper and photocopy one for each child. Alternatively, photocopy a larger outline on A3 paper for children to work on in pairs or small groups. Alphabet books or illustrated dictionaries would be useful for today's independent activity.

  You will also need a box with a lid (such as a shoe box), containing a toy animal, a piece of jewellery or any other object of interest.

- Day 4: you will need flashcards featuring the high frequency words, *a, and, at, in, of, on, the, up* and *was* (see Skills Masters 121–123).

DAY 1

Starter Level Big Book C pp. 4–7; Skills Master 81

Shared reading

- Ask a child to point to the title *A Dark, Dark Tale* on page 4 of Starter Level Big Book C.

- Read pages 4 to 7, emphasising the repetitive, poetic structure. Are the children surprised by the ending?

- Ask a child to point out the word that is printed in capital letters on page 7. Can they explain why *A MOUSE* is printed in this way? Re-read this page together, placing greater emphasis on the phrase, *A MOUSE*.

- What animals can the children see in Ruth Brown's illustrations?

Focused word/sentence work

- Slowly say the word *box*, and ask the children to identify each of the separate phonemes. Invite a child to write the word on the board. Underline the vowel and ask the class to tell you the sound it makes.

- Write more CVC words on the board for the class to read: *tap, pat, hip, map, cat, fix, hut, nut*. Now rub out the vowel in each word and replace it with the letter *o*. Ask children to read the new words you have made.

- Look at the words you have made. Can the children find words that rhyme with *top* (*hop, mop*); *pot* (*cot, hot, not*)? Can they think of a word in Ruth Brown's story that rhymes with *fox*? (*box*) Challenge the class to think of more words that contain the short vowel *o*.

Guided/independent work

- Skills Master 81 focuses on CVC words containing *o*.

Plenary

- Challenge the children to help you write the words *top*, *hop*, *mop*, *pot*, *cot*, *hot* and *not*, by identifying the separate phonemes as you slowly say the words.

- Provide an extension activity for more able children: ask them to listen as you say groups of CVC words and to tell you the word that does not contain the short vowel *o*. For example: *hat*, *hot*, *cot*; *top*, *tip*, *mop*.

DAY 2

Starter Level Big Book C pp. 4–7

Shared reading

- Re-read the story on pages 4 to 7, pausing for children to read key words, high frequency words and words that follow the pattern of the story. Encourage the children to use a range of strategies, such as picture clues, initial letter cues and awareness of the grammar of a sentence, to predict words.

- Ask the children to suggest different ways in which the author could have ended this tale. What else might there have been in the box?

- Can they think of other dark places that would make a good setting for a story?

Focused word/sentence work

- Ask the class to remind you of what was in the box at the end of Ruth Brown's story. What phoneme can they hear at the beginning of the word *mouse*?

- Demonstrate how to write the letter *m* on the board for the children to air trace. Compare the shape and size of lower and upper case *m* and *M* on an alphabet frieze.

- Using the box of items you have prepared (see Preparation), take out all of the items and look at each one in turn. Write the letter *m* on the outside of the box and ask the class to help you decide which items may go back in the box (i.e. those beginning with *m*).

Guided/independent work

- Give each child a mouse outline (see Preparation) in which to draw pictures of things beginning with *m*. Ask them to label each item with the letter *m*.

- Encourage more able children to write whole words beginning with *m*. Remind children of the items that belong in the *m* box.

- They may also use alphabet books or friezes, children's names (remembering to begin these with a capital *M*) and illustrated dictionaries.

Plenary

- Play a circle game. Hide something, such as a toy animal, a piece of jewellery or another object of interest inside a box (see Preparation). Don't let the children know what is inside the box. Pass it around and ask each child to say "Inside the dark, dark box there was a … ". Ask them each to try to think of something different.

- When each child has had a go, ask one child to open the box and take out the object inside. Ask the class to describe the object to you. Did anyone successfully guess what was inside?

DAY 3

Starter Level Big Book C p. 4

Shared writing

- Decide upon a repetitive theme to explore within a piece of shared creative writing. In place of the repeated word *dark*, you could use a word such as *old*, *huge*, *tiny*, *crooked*, *scary*.

- Turn to page 4 to remind the children of the words that Ruth Brown used to begin her tale. Begin your story with the same words "Once upon a time … ". You may like to use a computer to draft the shared writing, using a pre-cursive font. This would demonstrate how ICT can be used in the writing process. Make sure all the children can see the screen.

- Draw different ideas from the class to build up your own patterned tale. For example:

  Once upon a time there was an old, old palace.
  In the palace there was an old, old, hall.
  In the hall there was an old, old throne.
  Under the throne there was an old, old chest.
  In the chest there was a …

- Encourage the children to help you spell CVC words and simple high frequency words.

Focused word/sentence work

- Encourage the class to re-read the tale you have written together and think whether there is anything that they would like to change. Are all the children happy with the ending that has been chosen?

Guided/independent work

- If you used a computer to draft the shared writing, insert a page break between each line of the story and print it out. If there are thirty children in your class and your tale is six lines long, print the complete story out five times. (Alternatively, handwrite the lines and photocopy the required number of pages.) This will provide each child with a page featuring a line from the tale. Make sure each child knows what their line says (it may help to sit children with the same lines together). Ask them to carefully copy the sentence, and illustrate it.

- Explain that the sheets will all be displayed together, in the right order, to create an illustrated wall story.

- Alternatively, reproduce each line of the poem on a large sheet of card for a group of children to illustrate using colouring, paint or collage materials.

Plenary

- If children worked individually, arrange them with their illustrated lines in groups, so that each group has a complete story between them. Challenge them to sort the lines of the story into the right order. (If you used large sheets of card to produce one class story, carry out this activity as a whole class.)

- Encourage the class to try to re-read the story they have written collectively.

- Display the class story on a wall. If the children have produced several illustrated versions of the story between them, choose the best to display on the wall.

- Assemble the remaining stories into books, which may be used for group or independent reading.

DAY 4

**Starter Level Big Book C pp. 4–7;
Skills Masters 82 and 121–123**

Shared reading

- Re-read the story on pages 4 to 7 of Starter Level Big Book C, pausing for children to read key words, high frequency words and words that follow the pattern of the story.

Focused word/sentence work

- Using flashcards (see Preparation) ask the children to read the high frequency words *a*, *and*, *at*, *in*, *of*, *on*, *the*, *up* and *was*. Challenge them to find each of these words in the story on pages 4–7.

Guided/independent work

- Skills Master 82 is a cloze activity, exploring alternative endings for *A Dark, Dark Tale*.

Plenary

- Write the word *box* on the board. Ask the children to identify the three phonemes and tell you the letter names. Explain that you are going to play a game using the letters *o* and *x*.
- Draw a grid of nine squares on the board and teach the class how to play Noughts and Crosses, using the letters *o* and *x*. If you are using a metal board, use magnetic letters.
- Or remind the children of how to form the letter shapes and invite those taking a turn to write the appropriate letter in their chosen square. (Refer to the letters *o* and *x* rather than noughts and crosses.)

DAY 5

Starter Level Big Book C pp. 4–7; Skills Master 83

Shared reading

- Re-read the story on pages 4 to 7, pausing for children to read key words, high frequency words and words that follow the pattern of the story.
- Close the Big Book and see if the children can recite the patterned story from memory with prompts from you.

Focused word/sentence work

- Say the word *box* to the class and ask them to identify the final phoneme. Invite a child to write the letter that makes this phoneme on the board. What is its sound?
- Demonstrate the correct way to form this letter, and ask the children to air trace the shape or finger trace it on a nearby surface, such as the floor or a table top.
- Write the following words on the board: *axe*, *box*, *exit*, *fox*, *mix*, *six*. Give clues to these words containing the letter *x*, e.g. "an animal that looks like a dog with a bushy tail"; "a number"; "something used to chop wood".
- Once the children have given you the correct answer to each word, ask them to identify it on the board.

Guided/independent work

- Skills Master 83 focuses on the words containing *x* that were studied during today's focused word/sentence work session.

Plenary

- Re-read the "Once upon a time …" story that the class wrote and illustrated together on Day 3.

Consolidation and extension

- Skills Master 84 features another patterned picture story, based on the fairytale Jack and the Beanstalk, for the children to attempt to read independently.
- Re-read *A Dark, Dark Tale* by Ruth Brown, in its entirety. Look in detail at the full range of illustrations and discuss the themes that run through them.
- Find the author's name on the cover, spine and title page. Talk about her dual role as author and illustrator.

Unit 22 — People Who Help Us

Key Learning Objectives

TL1 Through shared reading:
a) to recognise printed and handwritten words in a variety of settings, e.g. signs, notices, letters

TL6 To re-read frequently a variety of familiar texts, e.g. big books, information books, own and other children's writing

TL11 Through shared writing:
a) to understand that writing can be used for a range of purposes, e.g. to send messages, inform

TL12 Through guided and independent writing:
a) to experiment with writing in a variety of play, exploratory and role-play situations
b) to write their own names

TL15 To use writing to communicate in a variety of ways, incorporating it into play and everyday classroom life

WL2 Knowledge of grapheme/phoneme correspondences through:
a) hearing and identifying initial sounds in words
b) reading letter(s) that represent(s) the sound(s): *d, f, p, sh, th*
c) writing each letter in response to each sound: *d, f, p, sh, th*
d) identifying and writing initial and dominant phonemes in spoken words

WL4 To link sound and spelling patterns by:
a) using knowledge of rhyme to identify families of rhyming CVC words
b) discriminating "onsets" from "rimes" in speech and spelling
c) identifying alliteration in known and new and invented words

WL5 To read on sight a range of familiar words

WL6 To read on sight the 45 high frequency words to be taught by the end of YR

WL11 To make collections of personal interest or significant words and words linked to particular topics

SL4 To use a capital letter for the start of own name

Range:	Simple non-fiction text
Texts:	*People at Work*, Karina Law *In the Street* (illustration)
Resources:	Starter Level Big Book C pp. 8–11 Skills Masters 85–88 and 124 or 125

High frequency words

a, and, are, can, day, for, in, look, the, they, to

Core activities

- Ensure that each child has a turn at role-playing in the class post office (see Day 2). Encourage them to incorporate writing into their play: filling in forms, writing messages, addressing envelopes, etc.

- Provide materials in the writing corner for making thank you cards and writing thank you letters.

- Using the three hoops labelled *d*, *f* and *p* and the collection of items beginning with those letters (see Day 2), ask all the children, in small groups or pairs, to sort the items into the correct hoops.

Preparation

- Day 1: you will need a toy telephone for a role-play situation, and, if possible, a walkie-talkie, a helmet and a stethoscope.

- Day 2: set up a class post office. Include a post box (ideally one made by the children), envelopes, stamps, a couple of post bag, forms, etc.

  You will need a plain card for each child to write a letter on. You will also need a collection of items beginning with *d*, *f* and *p*, and three hoops labelled *d*, *f* or *p*.

- Day 3: less able children could use Skills Master 3 – a template for a thank you card used in Unit 1 – to help them with today's independent activity.

DAY 1

Starter Level Big Book C pp. 8–10; Skills Master 85

Shared reading

- Read the unit title on page 8 of Starter Level Big Book C. Ask the class to think of people who help them in school, e.g. teachers, headteacher, classroom assistants, lunchtime supervisors, school administrators.

- Ask the children to think of people who help them outside of school, e.g. parents, grandparents, au pairs/childminders, doctors, nurses, dentists, shop assistants, librarians, police, firefighters.

- Ask the children to identify the people who help us in the photographs on pages 8, 9 and 10.

- Read the captions alongside each of the pictures. Talk about the emergency services. What telephone number should the children dial if ever they need a police officer, firefighter or ambulance in an emergency?

Focused word/sentence work

- What phoneme can the children hear at the beginning of the words *firefighter, police, ambulance, hospital, nurse, doctor*?

- Invite children to role-play the different people they can see on pages 8 and 9 of Starter Level Big Book C (if possible, provide appropriate accessories and props, e.g. a walkie-talkie, a helmet, a stethoscope).

- Ask them to tell the rest of the class what their work involves, e.g. "driving a fire engine", "wearing a special uniform", "wearing breathing apparatus", "using special equipment such as ladders and hoses".

- Prompt the rest of the class to ask questions. As the children use specialist vocabulary, e.g. *hose, fire engine, helmet*, write the words on the board.

- When the role-playing is over, read out some of the words randomly and ask the class to tell you which of the characters used them.

Guided/independent work

- Skills Master 85 reinforces words introduced on pages 8–10 of Starter Level Big Book C. Encourage children to focus on the initial letters and shape of each word as they try to match the words and pictures.

Plenary

- Using a toy telephone, role-play with the class what they should do in an emergency. Ask a child to dial 999 on the telephone and ask for the police, fire or hospital emergency service.
- Ask the child who has made the emergency call to tell you their name and address. Do all the children in your class know their addresses?
- Stress to children that they should only call 999 in a real emergency.

DAY 2

Starter Level Big Book C pp. 8–10; Skills Master 86

Shared reading

- Ask the class to identify the people depicted on pages 8–10 before re-reading the information text.
- Ask the children to talk about what they would like to do when they grow up.
- Talk about the postman on page 10 and the work that he does. Have the children ever received letters, cards or packages in the post? How did the postman or woman know where to deliver it?
- How many children know their own addresses? Remind the class of the importance of knowing where they live, and discuss the different reasons why.

Focused word/sentence work

- Divide the class into three groups: doctors, firefighters and police. Write the letters *d*, *f* and *p* on the board. Ask the children to tell you the sounds that these letters make. Which of these letters starts the words *doctor*, *firefighter* and *police*?
- Place three hoops labelled *d*, *f* or *p* on the floor. Give each child a plain piece of card and ask them to write the initial letter *d*, *f* or *p*, depending on which group they are in.
- Hold up each of your items in turn and ask the children holding cards with the corresponding initial letter to hold them in the air.
- Choose a "doctor", "firefighter" or "police officer" to then place the item in the correct hoop.

Guided/independent work

- Skills Master 86 provides an envelope template for the children to address to themselves. Ask them to put their own names and addresses on the front.
- Write the name of your village, town or city on the board. Who can tell you the name of the county you live in?
- When the envelopes have been addressed, children can cut out the envelopes and swap them with a friend who can write them a message on the reverse side. Encourage them to keep their messages secret for the time being.

Plenary

- Set up a class post office. Talk to the children about what they will need in their post office, e.g. a post box, envelopes, stamps, a post bag.
- Ask the children to post the addressed "envelopes", with their secret messages (completed during the independent session) into the post box. Give "postbags" to a couple of children and ask them to collect the envelopes from the "post box" and deliver them to the children whose names they bear.
- The children may then read the message written to them by a friend on the reverse side of their envelope.

DAY 3

Starter Level Big Book C pp. 8–10

Shared writing

- Ask the children to think of somebody in the school who helps them, such as a cook, lunchtime supervisor, caretaker or secretary.
- Draft a letter together thanking that person for all that they do. (Ideally, draft the letter on the computer, making sure all the children can see the screen. Alternatively, type or write out the letter at a later stage.)
- How would the children like to begin the letter? Prompt them to think specifically of the things that they appreciate about the chosen person. How would they like to finish the letter?
- Once the letter has been finished, encourage the class to read it with you. Let them make any changes that they think would improve the letter.
- Print the letter out and ask all the children to sign it. Invite a couple of children to decorate the letter and present it to the chosen person in front of the class.

Focused word/sentence work

- Write the words *thank you* on the board. Who can read what you have written? What phoneme can the children hear at the beginning of the word *thank*? Underline the letters *th*. Challenge the class to think of other words that begin with this phoneme, e.g. *theatre, thief, thing, think, thirsty, thousand, three, throat, throw, thumb, thunder, Thursday*.
- Does anyone have the *th* phoneme in their name? (e.g. *Beth*) If so, invite them to write their names on the board and underline the *th* phoneme.

Guided/independent work

- Ask each child to think of someone that they would like to say thank you to, e.g. a relative, childminder, nurse, doctor, teacher or friend.
- Give them an opportunity to write a thank you letter or make a thank you card. (Less able children could use Skills Master 3: a template for a thank you card used in Unit 1.)

Plenary

- Invite children to show and read their thank you letters and cards to the rest of the class. Give them time, in pairs, to look at and read each other's cards and letters.
- Re-read pages 8–10 of Starter Level Big Book C. Prompt children to read key words and high frequency words.

DAY 4

Starter Level Big Book C pp. 8–10; Skills Master 87

Shared reading

- Re-read pages 8–10 of Starter Level Big Book C. Prompt the children to read key words and high frequency words without your help.

Focused word/sentence work

- Write the phoneme *th* on the board and ask the children to remind you of the sound that these letters make.
- Say a number of words including some that contain *th*, e.g. *bath, birthday, brother, moth, nothing, path, the, then, this, thousand, three, thunder, tooth*. Ask the children to put their thumbs up when they hear a word containing *th*, and down when they hear a word that does not.
- Make up *th* tongue twisters, for example, "thirty-three thrushes".

Guided/independent work

- Skills Master 87 focuses on the *th* phoneme.

Plenary

- Repeat the thumb game you played during today's focused word/sentence work session: say a number of words including some that contain the *th* phoneme. Ask the children to put their thumbs up when they hear a word containing *th*, and down when they hear a word that does not.

DAY 5

Starter Level Big Book C p. 11; Skills Master 124 or 125

Shared reading

- Look at the street scene on page 11. Ask the class to point out all the people they can find who are doing something to help the community, including a police officer, lollipop lady, ambulance driver, postal worker and bus driver.
- Pick out the different street signs for the children to identify or read, e.g. a road sign, street name, shop sign, "for sale" sign, bus number.

Focused word/sentence work

- Say the word *shop*. What sound can the children hear at the beginning of this word?
- Write the word *shop* on the board and underline the *sh* phoneme. Which letter would the children need to change to make the word *stop*?
- Rub out the onset *s* and leave the rime *-op*. Challenge the children to think of different onsets to make non-words and words that rhyme with *shop* and *stop*, e.g. *hop, mop, pop*.

Guided/independent work

- Using a word wheel or word slide (see Skills Master 124 or 125), challenge the children to make words using the rime *-op*. Write the onsets *h, m, p, sh* and *st*. Encourage the children to record the words they make.

Plenary

- Play I Spy using the street scene on page 11 of Starter Level Big Book C. Who can find something beginning with *a* (ambulance), *b* (bus), *c* (car) and *d* (driver)?

Consolidation and extension

- Skills Master 88 focuses on signs the children are likely to encounter in the street.
- Make a display showing "people who help us" in your community. You may like to begin with a picture gallery of people who help you in your school/class. Include parents who come in to help.
- Invite a visitor from the community (e.g. a police officer, firefighter or paramedic) into the classroom to talk to the children and answer questions about their work.
- Take the children to observe a street outside, or near to, the school. What can they see? Who can they see at work? What signs can they identify/read?
- Teach the children rhymes with a *th* focus, e.g. I Hear Thunder, and tell them stories, e.g. Thumbelina by Hans Christian Anderson.

Unit 23   Little Sisters

Key Learning Objectives

TL4	To notice the difference between spoken and written forms through re-telling known stories
TL6	To re-read frequently a variety of familiar texts, e.g. big books, story books, taped stories with texts, poems
TL11	Through shared writing: f) to apply knowledge of the letter/sound correspondences in helping the teacher to scribe, and re-reading what the class has written
TL15	To use writing to communicate in a variety of ways, incorporating it into play and everyday classroom life, e.g. menus
WL2	Knowledge of grapheme/phoneme correspondences through: a) hearing and identifying initial sounds in words b) reading letter(s) that represent(s) the sound(s): *ch, qu, s* c) writing each letter in response to each sound: *qu, s* e) identifying and writing initial and final phonemes in consonant-vowel-consonant (CVC) words
WL4	To link sound and spelling patterns by: c) identifying alliteration in known and new and invented words
WL6	To read on sight the 45 high frequency words to be taught by the end of YR
SL2	To use awareness of the grammar of a sentence to predict words during shared reading and when re-reading familiar stories.

Range:	Poem and story with predictable structures
Texts:	From *The Baked Bean Queen*, Rose Impey *It's Time for Lunch, Rosie!* Tony Bradman, Collins
Resources:	Starter Level Big Book C pp. 12–17 Skills Masters 89–92 Listen-along Cassette Tracks 16 and 17, and Read-along Book pp. 48–53

High frequency words

a, all, and, away, dad, for, I, in, is, it, me, mum, my, no, on, play, she, the, to, up, we, you

Core activities

- Ask each child to re-read *The Baked Bean Queen* by Rose Impey, and *It's Time for Lunch, Rosie!* by Tony Bradman, using the Listen-along Cassette (Tracks 16 and 17) and Read-along Book (pp. 48–53).
- Set up a "kitchen" in the role-play area. Provide utensils for the children to re-enact the story of *The Baked Bean Queen*. Encourage children to read the menus they write on Day 3 to the "little sister" in their role-play, to see whether she approves.

- Ask each child to make the shapes *s* and *q* using modelling dough, a sand tray or finger paints.
- Using your sack full of items (see Preparation and Day 3) ask children, in pairs or small groups, to sort items beginning with *s* into a hoop labelled *s*.
- Provide materials for the children to make their own sock puppets. Ask them to think of names for their puppets, beginning with *S*. Encourage them to incorporate their puppets in their word play activities.

Preparation

- Days 2 and 3: you will need a sock puppet, made to resemble a snake by attaching two eyes and a forked tongue.
- Day 2: you will also need to provide each child or pair of children with the following plastic, magnetic or foam letters, or letter cards: *e, i, m, n, s, t, u* and *x*.
- Day 3: you will also need a hoop labelled *s* and a sack full of items, most of which begin with *s*, e.g. scissors, soap, a sock, a spider, string, sweets.
- Day 5: draw a large plate shape on an A4 sheet, leaving space around the edge of the plate to add labels. Photocopy one for each child.

DAY 1

Starter Level Big Book C pp. 12–13; Skills Master 89

Shared reading

- Read the unit title on page 12 of Starter Level Big Book C. How many children in your class have a little sister?
- Introduce the story extract from *The Baked Bean Queen* by Rose Impey. Talk about the pictures on page 12. What is the little girl in the high chair eating?
- Read the text on pages 12 and 13, pausing before the high frequency word *No!* on page 13 to see if the children can read it on their own.
- What is The Baked Bean Queen doing with her baked beans and sausages in the final picture on page 13?

Focused word/sentence work

- Point to the unit title on page 12 again and ask the class to read it to you. What sound can they hear at the beginning of the word *sisters*? How many times does the letter *s* appear in the word *sisters*? Can anyone find a word that begins with *s* on page 13? (*sausages*)
- Model the correct way to write the letter *s* on the board for the children to air trace and finger trace on a nearby surface.
- Sit the children in a circle. Take a ball of string and hold onto one end. Say a word beginning with *s*, e.g. *string*, then pass the ball of string on to a child whilst still holding the end. Continue in this way, asking each child who can think of a word beginning with *s* to hold onto the string before passing the ball on.

- After a while, ask the children to rewind the string. As they do so, ask the rest of the class to recall the word that each child gave, as he or she receives the ball of string again. Continue in this way until you are holding the ball of string once more.

Guided/independent work

- Skills Master 89 focuses on the letter *s*.

Plenary

- Repeat the string activity you introduced during today's focused word/sentence work session.

DAY 2

Starter Level Big Book C pp. 12–15

Shared reading

- Re-read pages 12–13, encouraging the children to join in where they can. Talk about the pictures on pages 14 and 15. Read the text on pages 14 and 15, pausing for the class to predict parts of the text, e.g. "No!" and "I love baked beans."
- Ask the questions in the "To think and talk about" box on page 15.

Focused word/sentence work

- Ask the class to help you spell some words beginning with *s*. Choose CVC words, such as *sad*, *set*, *sip*, *sit*, *six*, *sum* and *sun*. Write the initial letter *s* each time and ask the class to listen and tell you the next two phonemes that they hear, in order to complete the spelling of the words.
- Once a word has been completed, repeat it slowly for the class to judge whether it has been written correctly.

Guided/independent work

- Provide the children with the letters *e*, *i*, *m*, *n*, *s*, *t*, *u* and *x* (see Preparation) to build the words *set*, *sit*, *six*, *sum* and *sun* for themselves.

Plenary

- Introduce the children to your sock puppet, Sylvester Snake (see Preparation). Ask the children to tell you the sound that snakes make. (*Ssss*)
- Tell the class that Sylvester Snake loves to spell, but that he's not very good at it. Using the CVC words that you studied during the focused word/sentence work session, tell the class that Sylvester is going to help you spell some words. Ask the class to think of words they helped to spell earlier for Sylvester to try.
- Pretend that Sylvester is telling you the letters he thinks make up the words that are suggested, and write these on the board for him. Make one deliberate error in each word for the class to spot, for example: *sid* instead of *sad*; *sit* instead of *set*; *sik* instead of *six*; *fun* instead of *sun*.

DAY 3

Skills Master 90

Shared writing

- Ask the children to help you write a menu that they think would appeal to The Baked Bean Queen. Find out what foods they like best and list them for consideration.

Focused word/sentence work

- Show the class your sack full of items (see Preparation). Using your sock puppet (see Day 2), use Sylvester Snake to take each item out of the bag in turn.
- Ask the class to decide whether the item begins with Sylvester's favourite sound (*ssss*). If it does, Sylvester can put it into a hoop labelled *s*.

Guided/independent work

- Skills Master 90 is a decorative template for the children to write their own menu to tempt a fussy little sister. Talk about the illustrations to stimulate ideas.

Plenary

- Repeat the spelling game, with Sylvester Snake, which you played on Day 2.

DAY 4

Starter Level Big Book C pp. 12–15; Skills Master 91

Shared reading

- Ask the class to re-tell the story of *The Baked Bean Queen*. Compare their spoken version with the actual text on pages 12–15. Talk about the differences.

Focused word/sentence work

- Point to the story extract title on page 12 again, and ask the class to read it to you. What do they notice about the words *Baked Bean*? (Point out the alliteration and note the capital letter shape, *B*.)
- What sound can they hear at the beginning of the word *Queen*? Compare the upper and lower case letter shapes of *Q* and *q* on an alphabet frieze. Point out that, in English words, the letter *q* is always followed by a *u*.
- Help the children to think of other words that begin with *qu-*, e.g. *quack*, *question*, *quick*, *quiet*, *quilt*, *quiz*.
- Model the correct way to write *qu* on the board for the children to air trace and finger trace on a nearby surface.

Guided/independent work

- Skills Master 91 focuses on the phoneme *qu*.

Plenary

- Say the following words slowly and ask the class to think of a word beginning with *qu* that rhymes with each: *stick*, *back*, *whiz*, *bean*.
- Read the extract from *The Baked Bean Queen* on pages 12–15 one more time. Now that the children are more familiar with the text, prompt them to join in with key phrases.

DAY 5

Shared reading

- Introduce the poem *It's Time for Lunch, Rosie!* by Tony Bradman on pages 16 and 17. Talk about the illustrations, then read the poem to the class, pointing to each word as you do so.
- Ask the questions in the "To think and talk about" box.

Focused word/sentence work

- Focus on the word *Lunch* in the title of the poem. What sound do the letters *ch* make. Can the children recall any other words that begin or end with *ch*?
- Find and read the rhyming words in the poem: *spoon/soon; eat/feet; tray/away; say/play*. Can the children think of other words that rhyme with these pairs?
- Re-read the poem *It's Time for Lunch, Rosie!*, asking the class to listen out for the *s* phoneme. Emphasise the phoneme in the words *spoon, sitting, soon, something, spread, smear, say*.
- Pick out high frequency words and CVC words, e.g. *bib, cup, mix*, for children to read.

Guided/independent work

- Provide each child with a plate template (see Preparation). Ask them to remember what they had for lunch today or yesterday and draw each item on the plate. Help them to label each item on their plates.
- Find time for children to compare their plates of food with a friend and read each other's food labels.

Plenary

- Play Simple Simon Says. Adapt the game, using your sock puppet (see Preparation) to Sylvester Snake Says.
- Make up alliterative tongue twisters using the *s* phoneme.

Consolidation and extension

- Skills Master 92 features a picture based on the theme of this week's unit. It may be used for discussion purposes and for guided writing.
- Read the picture book story *The Baked Bean Queen* by Rose Impey in its entirety.
- Make a class collection of other stories and poems about little brothers.
- Use the plates that the children completed on Day 5 for the basis of an art project. Help them to recreate their lunches on paper plates using collage materials and paints. Help them to use a computer to make labels for their lunches.

Unit 24 Dragons

Key Learning Objectives

TL6 To re-read frequently a variety of familiar texts, e.g. big books, story books, poems, own and other children's writing

TL9 To be aware of story structures, e.g. actions/ reactions, consequences, and the ways that stories are built up and concluded

TL11 Through shared writing:
a) to understand that writing can be used for a range of purposes, e.g. to send messages, tell stories
f) to apply knowledge of letter/sound correspondences in helping the teacher to scribe, and re-reading what the class has written

TL12 Through guided and independent writing:
a) to experiment with writing in a variety of play and role-play situations

WL2 Knowledge of grapheme/phoneme correspondences through:
a) hearing and identifying initial sounds in words
b) reading letter(s) that represent(s) the sound(s): *d*
c) writing each letter in response to each sound: *d*
d) identifying and writing initial and dominant phonemes in spoken words
e) identifying and writing initial and final phonemes in consonant-vowel-consonant (CVC) words

WL3 Alphabetic and phonic knowledge through:
a) sounding and naming each letter of the alphabet in lower and upper case
c) understanding alphabetical order through alphabet books, rhymes, and songs

WL6 To read on sight the 45 high frequency words to be taught by the end of YR

Range:	Story with predictable structure; modern rhyme
Texts:	From *Alexander and the Dragon*, Katharine Holabird
	Our Dragon, Wendy Larmont
Resources:	Starter Level Big Book C pp. 18–24 Skills Masters 93–96

High frequency words

a, all, and, are, at, can, come, for, he, I, in, is, it, of, on, my, said, the, to, up, was, went, you

Core activities

- Give each child an opportunity to make the shape *d* using modelling dough, a sand tray or finger paints.
- Using your collection of items (see Preparation and Day 4) set children, in pairs or small groups, the task of sorting items beginning with *d* into the hoop labelled *d*.
- Turn the role-play area into a dragon's cave for children to use in their role-play. Try to make the cave dark.
- Place "dragon footprints" around the classroom. Encourage the children to leave messages for the dragon in its cave.

- Give the children more dragon shapes with letters of the alphabet on to sort into alphabetical order.

Preparation

- Day 2: you will need a complete set of lower and upper case letters. The children will need scissors to complete the guided/independent activity.
- Day 3: you will need enlarged copies of Skills Master 95 or an acetate copy, non-permanent pens and an overhead projector. You will also need a copy of Skills Master 94 enlarged to A3 size.
- Day 4: you will need a collection of objects, most of which begin with *d*, e.g. a dictionary, a die, a toy dinosaur, a dish, a toy dog, a doll, a dress, a drum, a toy duck; and a hoop labelled *d*.
- Day 5: you will need to provide each child or pair of children with the following plastic or foam letters, or letter cards: *b, d, e, n, r* and *t*.

DAY 1

Starter Level Big Book C pp. 18–19; Skills Master 93

Shared reading

- Open Starter Level Big Book C at pages 18 and 19. Help the class read the unit title, *Dragons*, by identifying each phoneme in turn until they are able to work out what it says.
- Look at the pictures on pages 18 and 19. What does it look as though the little boy on page 19 is doing?
- Read the title and the opening from *Alexander and the Dragon* by Katharine Holabird on pages 18–19.
- Encourage the class to talk about why they think Alexander was afraid of the dragon in his room. What would they do if they found a dragon under their bed?

Focused word/sentence work

- What phoneme can the children hear at the beginning of the word *dragon*?
- Revise the letter *d*, by comparing the lower and upper case shapes and asking the children to think of words beginning with *d*, e.g. *day, dentist, dig, dinosaur, doctor, dog, doll, donkey, draw, dress, drink, drum, duck*.
- Model how to write the letter *d* on the board for the class to air trace and then finger trace on a nearby surface.
- Say aloud three words that begin with *d* and one that does not, e.g. "dragon, door, sword, doughnut"; "dinosaur, lorry, duck, daisy". Ask the children to listen and tell you the word that does not begin with *d* in each instance.

Guided/independent work

- Skills Master 93 focuses on the letter *d*.

Plenary

- Write two letters on the board for the children to complete in different ways, e.g. –*ad* (*bad, dad, had, mad, pad, sad*); *di–* (*did, dig, dim, din, dip*); *do–* (*dog, dot*). Accept non-words that are correctly pronounced according to the spelling pattern.

Shared reading

- Open Starter Level Big Book C at pages 18 and 19 and ask the class to re-tell the story extract so far. Turn to pages 20 and 21 and ask the children to tell you what is happening in the pictures. Do they think that the dragon looks fierce?

- Can the children read the first word, in upper case letters, on page 20? Why is it in upper case letters and how should it be read?

- Read the text on pages 20 and 21. What do the children think will happen next?

- Read the conclusion to the story extract on pages 22 and 23.

- What made Alexander change his mind about fighting the dragon? Do the children think Alexander and the dragon will remain friends?

Focused word/sentence work

- Ask the children to tell you the boy's name in the story extract. Write *Alexander* on the board. What sound does the first letter make? What is the letter name? Ask a child to write a lower case *a* in order to compare the shapes. Can they tell you where in the alphabet the letter *a* comes?

- What sound can the children hear at the beginning of *dragon*? Where in the alphabet does the letter *d* come? (Refer to an alphabet frieze.) What is the last letter of the alphabet?

- Hand out a complete set of lower case letters to the children. Slowly say the alphabet and ask each child to hold up their letter as it is called.

- Repeat using upper case letters.

- Sing or recite the alphabet together.

Guided/independent work

- Skills Master 94 is a reinforcement activity for sequencing letters of the alphabet. The children will need scissors to complete the activity. They will need their dragons for a plenary activity.

Plenary

- Ask each child to choose one dragon from their guided/independent activity. (Alternatively, make copies of Skills Master 94: four copies will be enough for a class of 28 children. Cut out the dragons and give one to each child.) Ask the children to read the letter on their dragon and then hide it.

- They then walk around the classroom saying the phoneme aloud and group together with other children who are saying the same phoneme.

- Once the children have grouped together, ask them to show their dragons and check that they match. Keep the dragons safe for use on Day 3.

Shared writing

- Using enlarged copies of Skills Master 95 (or an acetate copy, non-permanent pens and an overhead projector), ask the children to look at the picture and think about what they would say if they found a dragon under their bed.

- Write a few different sentences, taking ideas from different children to show that there are a variety of ways in which a dragon might be approached: some friendly, some unfriendly.

- Re-read each sentence, asking the child who suggested it to confirm whether it represents what he or she was thinking.

Focused word/sentence work

- Using the dragons from Day 2 (see Plenary), repeat the matching phonemes game.

- The game may also be played with children saying the letter names rather than phonemes.

- Using an enlarged copy of Skills Master 94, hand out a complete set of dragons to seven children. Ask them to arrange themselves at the front of the class so that the letters spell *dragons*.

Guided/independent work

- Skills Master 95 is a writing frame for children to think about and write what they would say if they found a dragon under their bed.

Plenary

- Invite children who have completed the guided/independent activity to read or talk about their writing to the rest of the class.

- Using your enlarged copy of Skills Master 94, hand out a complete set of dragons to seven children (choose different children from those who took part during the focused word/sentence work session). Again, ask them to arrange themselves, with the help of the class, so that the letters spell *dragons*.

- Challenge them to spell other words with the letters, such as *an, drag, on, ran*.

Shared reading

- Re-read the story extract on pages 18–23, asking the children to listen for sentences that describe the dragon. How is it described? What colour is it? What colour are its teeth?

- Encourage the children to create imaginary words to describe the dragon.

Focused word/sentence work

- Revise the phoneme *d*. Compare the lower and upper case shapes and make the corresponding sound together.

- Using your collection of objects (see Preparation), ask the class to help you sort items beginning with *d* into the hoop labelled *d*.

Guided/independent work

- Ask the children to draw a dragon and write a sentence about it. Encourage them to show their drawings, and read their sentences to a partner, comparing details and talking about the differences.

Plenary

- Choose children to display their drawings and read their sentences to the rest of the class.

- How many of the children's dragons have wings? How many are breathing fire? How many are a colour other than green?

- Draw a simple outline of a dog on the board. Tell the children you have drawn a dragon. When they tell you that it looks like a dog, ask them to help you turn the dog into a dragon by giving instructions, e.g. "its tail should be longer"; "its claws should be bigger"; "it should have wings".

- Encourage the children to give you specific details and make their instructions clear.

DAY 5

Starter Level Big Book C p. 24

Shared reading

- Introduce the poem on page 24. Help the children to identify and read the title. Talk about the picture, then read through the poem.

- Ask the questions in the "To think and talk about" box.

Focused word/sentence work

- Ask the children to remind you of what was used to make the dragon's fiery breath. Encourage them to identify the separate phonemes in "red net" and write the words on the board.

- Tell the children that they are going to help you make a word chain that begins with *red* and ends with *net*.

- Rub out the word *net* and ask the children to tell you which letter to change to make *red* into *bed*. Which letter do they need to change to make *bed* into *bet*? Finally, what letter do they need to change to make *bet* into *net*?

Guided/independent work

- Provide the children with the letters *b*, *d*, *e*, *n*, *r* and *t* (see Preparation) to build the CVC words *red*, *bed*, *bet* and *net* for themselves.

Plenary

- Re-read the poem on page 24.

Consolidation and extension

- Skills Master 96 is a revision activity focusing on words beginning with *d*.

- Read the picture book story, *Alexander and the Dragon* by Katharine Holabird, in its entirety.

- Build a class dragon, using the poem on page 24 of Starter Level Big Book C as a guide. Record a dragon's roar on a tape recorder for the children to play back.

- Re-enact the story extract, *Alexander and the Dragon*, through role-play.

Unit 25 | Night Noises

Key Learning Objectives

TL6	To re-read frequently a variety of familiar texts, e.g. big books, story books, taped stories with texts, poems, own writing
TL11	Through shared writing: a) to understand that writing can be used for a range of purposes f) to apply knowledge of letter/sound correspondences in helping the teacher to scribe, and re-reading what the class has written
WL1	To understand and be able to rhyme through: a) recognising, exploring and working with rhyming patterns b) extending these patterns by analogy, generating new and invented words in speech and spelling
WL2	Knowledge of grapheme/phoneme correspondences through: e) identifying and writing initial and final phonemes in consonant-vowel-consonant (CVC) words
WL4	To link sound and spelling patterns by: a) using knowledge of rhyme to identify families of rhyming CVC words b) discriminating "onsets" from "rimes" in speech and spelling
WL6	To read on sight the 45 high frequency words to be taught by the end of YR
WL11	To make collections of personal interest or significant words and words linked to particular topics
SL2	To use awareness of the grammar of a sentence to predict words during shared reading and when re-reading familiar stories

Range:	Modern rhymes; story with predictable structure
Texts:	*Night Sounds*, Berlie Doherty, Collins From *Big Fat Hen and the Red Rooster*, Vivian French *Early Country Village Morning*, Grace Nichols
Resources:	Starter Level Big Book C pp. 25–31 Skills Masters 97–100, 121–123 and 124 or 125 Listen-along Cassette Tracks 18 and 19, and Read-along Book pp. 54–55

High frequency words

a, all, am, and, big, can, day, for, get, I, in, is, it, me, of, on, said, she, the, they, to, up, was, went, you

Core activities

- Give each child an opportunity to re-read *Night Sounds*, by Berlie Doherty, and *Early Country Village Morning*, by Grace Nichols, using the Listen-along Cassette (Tracks 18 and 19) and Read-along Book (pp. 54–55).

- Provide a set of farm animals, or animal masks, for children to re-enact the story extract from *Big Fat Hen and the Red Rooster*.

- Encourage them to continue the story through role-play.

- Use a word wheel or word slide (see Skills Master 124 or 125) to investigate the rimes *-ig* (e.g. *big, dig, jig, pig, wig*), *-at* (e.g. *bat, cat, fat, hat, mat, pat, sat*) and *-en* (e.g. *den, hen, men, pen, ten, then*).

Preparation

- Day 1: you will need the following flashcards (see Skills Masters 121–123): *all, and, can, for, I, in, is, it, me, on, the.*

- Day 3: prepare a set of flashcards featuring the words *hen, pig, sheep, cow, dog* and *cat.*

- Day 5: you will need the following flashcards (see Skills Masters 121–123): *a, and, big, of, the, they.*

DAY I

Starter Level Big Book C p. 25

Shared reading

- Introduce the poem by Berlie Doherty on page 25 of Starter Level Big Book C. Read the unit title and the title of the poem.

- Ask the class to talk about the picture: What time of day is it? Where is the little girl? Has she just gone to bed or is she about to get up? Which toys has she taken to bed with her?

- Read the poem slowly, pausing for children to predict or decode key words such as *bed*.

- Talk about the poem. What can the little girl hear from her bed?

- What other sounds do the children sometimes hear at night? For example, owls, a dog barking, the television in another room, cars, trains, voices, a baby crying, the wind or rain.

Focused word/sentence work

- Hold up the following flashcards (see Preparation) in turn and ask the class to read the words and find them in the poem on page 25: *all, and, can, for, I, in, is, it, me, on, the.*

- Ask the children to listen as you slowly say the word *bed*, and identify the separate phonemes. Ask a child to find this word in the poem on page 25. Can anyone think of a colour that rhymes with *bed*? (*red*)

- Read the last line of the poem once more, emphasising the *th* phoneme at the beginning of the words *then* and *think*. Ask the children what phoneme they hear at the beginning of these words.

- Write the letters *th* on the board and ask the children to think of more words beginning with *th*, e.g. *that, the, them, then, there, they, this, thousand, three, thumb, thunder.*

Guided/independent work

- Give the children a sentence opener to copy and complete: "In bed I can hear … "

Plenary

- Invite children to read their sentences to the rest of the class.

DAY 2

Starter Level Big Book C pp. 26–28; Skills Master 97

Shared reading

- Encourage the class to read the story title on page 26. What animals can they see on pages 26 and 27?
- Read the text on pages 26, 27 and 28, pausing for the class to supply the many CVC words and high frequency words for you. (Read it again for fluency.)
- Ask the class to demonstrate the noises, in bold text, made by the hen, rooster and pig.
- Ask the children what or who wakes them in the morning.

Focused word/sentence work

- Ask the class to identify the separate phonemes in the words *Big Fat Hen*. Choose children to write these words on the board.
- Taking each word in turn, help the class to find words that rhyme with each word, by changing the onsets. List them on the board under the words *Big Fat Hen*. Read each list together.

Guided/independent work

- Skills Master 97 requires children to spell words that rhyme with *big*, *fat* and *hen* by analogy.

Plenary

- Sing a revised version of Old MacDonald Had a Farm:

  Farmer Tile, she had a farm. E-I-E-I-O!
  And on that farm she had a hen. E-I-E-I-O!

  With a cluck, cluck, here,
  And a cluck, cluck, there.
  Here a cluck, there a cluck,
  Everywhere a cluck, cluck.
  Farmer Tile, she had a farm.
  E-I-E-I-O!

  Sing about the animals in the same order as the text, as follows: hen (*cluck, cluck*), pig (*oink, oink*), cow (*moo, moo*), sheep (*baa, baa*). The rooster is a challenge, but the children may have their own ideas about how he may be incorporated!

DAY 3

Skills Master 98 and 121–123

Shared writing

- Remind the children of the song they sang during Day 2's plenary session: Farmer Tile, She Had a Farm.
- Ask them to help you make up some new verses and to suggest more animals that could be included (they need not be typical farm animals). Write their suggested animals in a list on the board.
- Ask the children to think of an animal noise that could be used for each animal, and write this beside the animal. For example:

  dog – woof, woof
  cat – miaow
  horse – neigh, neigh
  snake – sssssssss
  goose – honk, honk

- Perform the new verses together, pointing to each animal name and sound on the board as you sing them.
- Where children have chosen animals and noises that don't fit the rhythm of the song, discuss ideas for resolving the problem or decide together to take them out of the song and erase the words.

Focused word/sentence work

- Hold up your flashcards with the words *hen, pig, sheep, cow, dog* and *cat* (see Preparation) at random.
- Ask the class to respond with the corresponding animal noise to show that they recognise the word you are displaying (*cluck, oink, baa, moo, woof* and *miaow*).
- Revise the rimes *-ig, -at,* and *-en*. Help the class to make rhyming strings using the words *big, fat* and *hen*. List their suggestions of rhyming words and non-words on the board and read each list together.

Guided/independent work

- Skills Master 98 focuses on animal names and noises. The children are required to link each animal name to its correct sound. Four of the animal sounds are words that the children have encountered in this unit's shared text.

Plenary

- Repeat your animal flashcards activity (see Focused word/sentence work). Change the game slightly, dividing the class into six groups and assigning an animal to each group.
- As you hold up each animal name, only the group to whom that animal has been assigned should make the animal's sound.
- Sing Farmer Tile, She Had a Farm again, incorporating the new verses written by the children in today's shared writing session.
- Invite volunteers to play the parts of the different animals, reminding the rest of the class to be silent when the volunteers step forward to make their animal sound.

DAY 4

Starter Level Big Book C pp. 26–30; Skills Master 99

Shared reading

- Ask the children to remind you of the story extract they read on pages 26–28. Look at the animals' thought bubbles on these pages and ask the children to remind you what each animal was dreaming about.
- Re-read pages 26–28, encouraging the children to join in where possible.
- Who is Big Fat Hen talking to on page 29? Read pages 29 and 30.

Focused word/sentence work

- Re-read the first two sentences on page 30. Point to the word *she* and ask the class to read it to you. What sound do the letters *sh* make? Can the children think of an animal in the story that begins with this phoneme? Who can point to the word *Sheep* on page 30?
- Encourage the class to think of more words beginning with *sh*, by giving them clues. For example, "a large boat" (*ship*); "something you might find on the seashore" (*shell*); "somewhere you go to buy things" (*shop*); "somewhere adults keep garden tools" (*shed*).
- Give clues to words that end with *sh*. For example, "something you use to make your hair neat" (*brush*); "an animal that lives in water" (*fish*).
- Ask the children to help you write the word *fish* on the board by identifying the separate phonemes.
- Rub out the *f* and replace with different letters for the children to read new non-words and words, e.g. *dish*, *wish*.

Guided/independent work

- Skills Master 99 focuses on the phoneme *sh*.

Plenary

- Recite alliterative tongue twisters using *sh* such as "She sells sea shells upon the seashore." Make up more *sh* tongue twisters of your own.

DAY 5

Starter Level Big Book C p. 31; Skills Masters 121–123

Shared reading

- Introduce the poem by Grace Nichols on page 31 of Starter Level Big Book C. Read the title and ask the class to talk about what they can see in the border illustrations.
- Read the poem slowly, pausing for children to predict or decode key words such as *hens, bus, sun*. Use the border illustrations to help children with words such as *donkey*.

- Talk about the poem. At what time of day does it take place? What early-morning sounds has the poet identified? Where does the title of the poem suggest the poem takes place?
- What sounds do the children hear early in the morning where they live? For example, milk or post being delivered, a dog barking, a cockerel, traffic, yawning, the kettle boiling, the radio.

Focused word/sentence work

- Help the class to identify the separate phonemes in *bus* and *sun*. Choose children to write these words on the board. Ask children to find these words in the poem on page 31.
- Help the class find non-words and words that rhyme with *sun*, by changing the onset. For example, *bun, fun, run*. List them on the board and read the list together.
- Hold up the following flashcards (see Preparation) in turn and ask the class to read the words and find them in the poem on page 31: *a, and, big, of, the, they*.

Guided/independent work

- Give the children a sentence opener to copy and complete: "In the morning I can hear … "

Plenary

- Invite children to read their sentences to the class.
- Re-read *Early Country Village Morning* by Grace Nichols on page 31 of Starter Level Big Book C, encouraging the class to join in where possible.

Consolidation and extension

- Skills Master 100 is a consolidation activity focusing on CVC words with the rimes -*en* and -*ig*.
- Take the children on a tour of the school and the school grounds to collect sounds. Take a tape recorder to record the sounds, then play them back in the classroom for the children to recall what sounds they heard.
- Make sound effects to accompany the poem on page 31 of Starter Level Big Book C: *Early Country Village Morning*, by Grace Nichols. Include cocks crowing, a donkey clip-clopping, a bus, yawning, plus any other sounds that the children think would be fitting. Use the sound effects to accompany the poem recital on the Listen-along Cassette.
- Read the picture story, *Big Fat Hen and the Red Rooster* by Vivian French, in its entirety.

The Yummy Alphabet

Key Learning Objectives

TL1	Through shared reading: a) to recognise printed and handwritten words in a variety of settings, e.g. labels, lists
TL12	Through guided and independent writing: b) to write their own names
TL15	To use writing to communicate in a variety of ways, incorporating it into play and eachday classroom life, e.g. lists, labels
WL2	Knowledge of grapheme/phoneme correspondences through: a) hearing and identifying initial sounds in words b) reading letter(s) that represent(s) the sound(s): *a–z, ch, sh, th* c) writing each letter in response to each sound: *a–z, ch, sh, th* d) identifying and writing initial and dominant phonemes in spoken words
WL3	Alphabetic and phonic knowledge through: a) sounding and naming each letter of the alphabet in lower and upper case b) writing letters in response to letter names c) understanding alphabetical order through alphabet books, rhymes, and songs
WL5	To read on sight a range of familiar words, e.g. children's names, captions, labels, and words from favourite books
WL8	To read and write own name and explore other words related to the spelling of own name
WL11	To make collections of words linked to particular topics
SL4	To use a capital letter for the start of own name.

Range:	Simple non-fiction text
Texts:	*The Yummy Alphabet*, Chris Lutrario, Collins Pathways
Resources:	Starter Level Big Book C pp. 32–37 Skills Masters 101–104

High frequency words

a, of, the

Core activities

- Provide a collection of alphabet books for the children to read and refer to.
- Set up a class grocery store or supermarket. Help to label the foods with their names and prices and put up signs. Provide shopping bags, pretend cheques to fill out and pretend money, for the children to role-play being customers and sales assistants. Encourage them to write shopping lists.
- Give children a complete set of lower case letters and a handful of upper case letters, using plastic, foam or magnetic letters or word cards. Ask them to find the lower case letters that correspond with each upper case letter.

- Give each child an opportunity, in pairs or small groups, to sequence the food items used on Day 2 in alphabetical order.

Preparation

- Day 1: you will need an alphabet frieze positioned at a height that is accessible to the children. You will also need a set of upper and lower case plastic or foam letters or letter cards.
- Day 2: you will need a collection of plastic food items for a sequencing activity; choose about eight foods that begin with different letters. Or use tinned or longlife foods that will endure a week of handling, e.g. a tin of baked beans, a carrot, an orange, a potato, a bag of salt.
- Day 4: you will need a piece of thin card for each child for them to write their name on.

  The children will need scissors for the guided/ independent activity.
- Day 5: you will need a set of upper and lower case plastic or foam letters or letter cards.

DAY I

Starter Level Big Book C pp. 32–34; Skills Master 101

Shared reading

- Read the title of the alphabet text that begins on page 32, *The Yummy Alphabet*, by Chris Lutrario. Ask the class to predict what this alphabet text is about.
- Focus on the letters above each picture on pages 32–34. Compare the shapes of the lower and upper case letters. Ask the children to tell you the sound that each letter makes and the letter name. Then see if they can identify the food beginning with that letter in the picture.
- Once you have focused on all the letters from Aa to Ll, go back to the beginning and read each of the words together: *apple, bread, crisps,* etc.

Focused word/sentence work

- Give each child a lower case letter. Call letters out randomly, using letter names rather than sounds. The child with the corresponding letter is to run to the alphabet frieze (see Preparation) and hold it against the correct letter to show that they match.
- Repeat the above activity using upper case letters. This game helps children to become familiar with the position of letters in the alphabet sequence. These skills will help them when they begin to use dictionaries more frequently as part of their literacy activities.
- Sing or recite the alphabet.

Guided/independent work

- Skills Master 101 features foods from *The Yummy Alphabet*, four of which were featured in today's shared reading session.
- Children write the initial letter next to each food. For children who are confident in identifying and writing lower case letters, ask them to write upper case letters.
- Keep the sheets safe for an extension activity on Day 2.

Plenary

- Call out, in order, the letters of the alphabet from *a* to *l*. See if the children are able to recall the food for each letter that was featured in *The Yummy Alphabet*.
- Repeat the frieze game that you played during today's focused word/sentence work session.

DAY 2

Starter Level Big Book C pp. 32–37; Skills Master 101 from Day 1

Shared reading

- Compare the shapes of the lower and upper case letters in pages 35–37 of *The Yummy Alphabet*. Ask the children to tell you the sound that each letter makes and the letter name.
- Then see if the children can identify the food beginning with that letter in the picture. For *x* and *z*, note that the phoneme appears at the end or in the middle of the word.
- Remind the class that there are not many words that begin with these letters.
- Once you have focused on all the letters from *Mm* to *Zz*, go back to the beginning and read all of the food words together: *apple*, *bread*, *crisps*, through to *fizzy drink*.

Focused word/sentence work

- Hand out the food items you have collected (see Preparation) to different children.
- Recite the alphabet slowly as a class. At each letter, check to see if any child is holding food beginning with that letter. As each letter is called, ask the children to stand at the front of the class with their foods, in alphabetical order.
- Ask the class to cover their eyes, then swap a few children in the line at the front of the class. Ask the class to uncover their eyes and recite the alphabet again. Ask the class to tell you who is now standing in the wrong place and where in the line they should move to.

Guided/independent work

- Using Skills Master 101 from Day 1, ask children to cut out each food box and then sequence them in alphabetical order, using the alphabet line at the bottom of the sheet for reference.

Plenary

- Repeat the sequencing game you played during today's word work session.

DAY 3

Skills Master 102

Shared writing

- Ask the children to remind you of some of the foods they saw in *The Yummy Alphabet*. Tell them that they are going to help you to write a shopping list of foods for a picnic, including some of the foods from *The Yummy Alphabet*, along with others that the children like.

- For each food that the children suggest, ask them to identify the phoneme at the beginning of the word to help you spell it.

Focused word/sentence work

- Write the name of one of the children in your class on the board. Who can read the name?
- Underneath, write the same name in capital letters and ask the class to tell you what it says. Ask them to explain the difference between the two names. Which letter in the first name is a capital letter?
- Rub out both names and write the same name vertically on the left-hand side of the board in upper case letters. Use a different colour for the letters of the child's name so that it stands out.
- Tell the class that they are going to write a list of foods beginning with the letters in that child's name, for example:

      Milk
      Egg
      Grapes
      Apple
      Nuts

  Find out from "Megan" which of the foods in her name she likes best. Next, use a name where one of the letters is repeated, and encourage the class to find different foods for the repeated letter/s. For example:

      Milk
      Orange
      Honey
      Apple
      Mushrooms
      Marmalade
      Egg
      Doughnut

Guided/independent work

- Set the children the task of writing a shopping list for a picnic using Skills Master 102. Talk about the illustrative border to stimulate ideas. More able children could be challenged to write foods beginning with the letters of their names (see Focused word/sentence work).

Plenary

- Repeat today's focused word work activity: write a list of foods beginning with the letters of a child's name.
- Give the children time to show each other their shopping lists in pairs.

DAY 4

Starter Level Big Book C pp. 32–37

Shared reading

- Re-read *The Yummy Alphabet* on pages 32–37 of Starter Level Big Book C.

Focused word/sentence work

- Sit the children in a circle. Ask each child, in turn, to say the phoneme at the start of their name. Once everybody has successfully done this, ask each child in turn to say the name of a food that begins with the same phoneme as their name.

- For children who get stuck, turn to the relevant letter on pages 32–37 to help them. Discuss other phonemes with the rest of the class, e.g. *Ch* for *Charlie* (chocolate).

Guided/independent work

- Provide each child with a piece of thin card on which to write their name clearly, reminding them to begin with a capital letter. They may like to use a different colour for each letter. Ask them to decorate the name card with a food or foods beginning with the same letter as their name.

- More able children may like to draw foods that begin with the different letters that make up their names. The names may be used as tray, book or peg labels, depending on the size of card you have provided.

Plenary

- Collect all the children's name cards. Holding up each card in turn, ask the children to remain silent when they recognise their own name card, then see if the other children are able to identify the familiar names of their classmates.

- Sing or recite the alphabet.

DAY 5

Starter Level Big Book C pp. 32–37; Skills Master 103

Shared reading

- Re-read *The Yummy Alphabet* on pages 32–37 of Starter Level Big Book C.

Focused word/sentence work

- Hand out a set of upper case letters to half the class and the corresponding lower case letters to the rest of the class. See how quickly the children are able to find their partners.

- Collect up the lower case letters, and then the upper case letters. Hand out the upper case letters to the children who were previously given lower case letters, and vice versa. Once again, see how quickly the children are able to find their partners.

Guided/independent work

- Skills Master 103 requires children to match upper and lower case letters.

Plenary

- Repeat the upper and lower case matching letter game you played during the focused word/sentence work session.

Consolidation and extension

- Skills Master 104 is an alphabet sequencing activity.

- Hang a low, string washing line across the room and attach 26 pegs. Collect, or ask the children to draw, pictures of foods beginning with each letter of the alphabet and give the children opportunities, in small groups, to peg the pictures to the washing line in the correct order.

- Move some of the pictures from time to time and see who can spot which pictures are in the wrong places.

- Make a class alphabet frieze. Assign each child with a letter of the alphabet. If there are more than 26 children in your class, let some children work in pairs. Ask each child to draw the corresponding food from *The Yummy Alphabet*, or another they have chosen beginning with the same letter, and label it with the initial letter in lower and upper case.

Unit 27 Working With Words

Key Learning Objectives

TL1 Through shared reading:
c) to understand and use correctly terms about books and print: *book, cover, beginning, end, page, line, word, letter, title*

WL2 Knowledge of grapheme/phoneme correspondences through:
a) hearing and identifying initial sounds in words
b) reading letter(s) that represent(s) the sound(s): *m, n*
c) writing each letter in response to each sound: *m, n*
d) identifying and writing initial and dominant phonemes in spoken words
e) identifying and writing initial and final phonemes in consonant-vowel-consonant (CVC) words

WL3 Alphabetic and phonic knowledge through:
a) sounding and naming each letter of the alphabet in lower and upper case
b) writing letters in response to letter names
c) understanding alphabetical order through alphabet books, rhymes, and songs

WL4 To link sound and spelling patterns by:
c) identifying alliteration in known and new and invented words

WL5 To read on sight a range of familiar words, e.g. children's names, captions, labels, and words from favourite books

Range:	Simple non-fiction text
Texts:	From *My ABC Dictionary*, Irene Yates, Collins
Resources:	Starter Level Big Book C pp. 38–43 Skills Masters 105–108

High frequency words

a, am, and, are, big, day, for, I, in, is, like, look, my, no, of, on, the, this, to, up, we, you

Core activities

- Ask each child, in pairs or small groups, to sort out your collection of items (see Preparation and Day 2) into two hoops labelled *m* and *n*.
- Provide modelling dough, a sand tray or finger paints for each child to make the shapes *m* and *n*.
- Using magnetic letters, set up an alphabet fishing game. Use only six consecutive letters at a time, e.g. *a–f*. Ask the children to fish them out in alphabetical order, using a paperclip tied to the end of a piece of string.

Preparation

- Day 1: make a collection of dictionaries and word books appropriate for the children in your class.
- Day 2: you will need a collection of items beginning with *m*, e.g. a magazine, a magnet, a map, marmalade, a mask, a toy mouse, a milk carton, a mirror, a toy

monkey, a mug; and *n*, e.g. nails, a net, a newspaper, nuts. You will also need two hoops, labelled *m* and *n*.
- Day 3: you will need a hand mirror and a newspaper (or two other items beginning with *m* and *n*).
- Day 4: you will need an alphabet frieze positioned at a height that is accessible to the children.
- Provide children, in pairs, with a selection of lower case letters and corresponding upper case letters, using foam, plastic or magnetic letters or letter cards.
- Day 5: if possible, gather a few dictionaries or word books with end pages featuring word lists for colours, numbers, shapes, opposites, animals, etc.

You will also need two sets of word cards:
Set 1: big, day, in, fat, dry, on, down, slow
Set 2: little, night, out, thin, wet, off, up, fast

DAY 1

Starter Level Big Book C pp. 38–39; Skills Master 105

Shared reading

- Show the children your collection of word books and dictionaries. Talk about the covers and identify the spine. Discuss the different uses of these books, and how they explain the meanings of words.
- Show and read the titles. Explain that the words appear in alphabetical order. What letter appears at the beginning? What letter is at the end? How many pages are there in each book?
- Introduce the dictionary extract on pages 38 and 39 of Starter Level Big Book C. Compare the shapes of the upper and lower case letters *M* and *m*. Find the letters *M* and *m* in the alphabet line at the bottom of the spread.
- Talk about the main picture and read the alliterative sentence that accompanies it.
- See if the class can identify the other illustrations in the spread, reminding them that all the pictures are there to illustrate words beginning with *m*.
- Read the definitions on pages 38 and 39.

Focused word/sentence work

- Close the Big Book and ask the children to tell you the phoneme they hear at the beginning of the word *mouse*.
- Ask a child to write the letter *m* on the board. Check to see that he or she forms the letter correctly. Ask the class to finger trace the shape in the air and on a nearby surface.
- Ask the children to think of other words that begin with the *m* phoneme, e.g. *magic, man, map, mask, May, milk, million, minute, mirror, mistake, Monday, money, monkey, monster, month, morning, mouth, mum, music*. Give clues to words that they do not think of for themselves.
- Ask the children to help you make word chains of CVC words beginning with *m* by listening carefully to each phoneme as you slowly say the words. Begin by asking them to tell you the phonemes they can hear in the word *mop*. Write each letter on the board as the children correctly tell you each phoneme they hear.

- Ask them which letter they need to change to turn *mop* into *map*, *map* into *mat* and *mat* into *met*?
- Ask the class to help you build another chain of CVC words beginning with *m*: *man* → *mad* → *mud* → *mug*.

Guided/independent work

- Skills Master 105 focuses on words beginning with *m*.

Plenary

- Write the letter *i* on the board and ask the class to tell you the initial and final phonemes they hear in the word *mix*. Write *m* and *x* either side of the vowel once the children have identified them. Repeat with *u* (*mud*, *mug*, *mum*), and *a* (*man*, *map*, *mat*).

DAY 2

Starter Level Big Book C pp. 40–41; Skills Master 106

Shared reading

- Introduce the dictionary extract on pages 40 and 41 of Starter Level Big Book C. Compare the shapes of the upper and lower case letters *N* and *n*. Find the letters *N* and *n* in the alphabet line at the bottom of the spread.
- Talk about the main picture and read the alliterative sentence that accompanies it. Help the class identify the other illustrations in the spread, reminding them that all the pictures are there to illustrate words beginning with *n*.
- Read the definitions on pages 40 and 41.

Focused word/sentence work

- Present your collection of items to the class (see Preparation) and ask them to help you sort them into two hoops labelled *m* and *n*.

Guided/independent work

- Skills Master 106 focuses on words beginning with *n*.

Plenary

- Say a number of words that begin with *n* and one that does not, and ask the class to tell you which of the words does not begin with *n*. For example, "no, newt, umbrella, November"; "name, nine, now, river".

DAY 3

Starter Level Big Book C pp. 38 and 40

Shared writing

- Look again at the alliterative sentences on pages 38 and 40. Encourage the children to help you write more alliterative sentences using the letters *m* and *n*. Explain that the sentences may be nonsensical. For example, "Naughty newts nicked Nan's newspaper."; "Monsters like to munch macaroni."

Focused word/sentence work

- Sit the class in a circle. Pass a hand mirror around the group and ask each child to say a word beginning with *m* before passing the mirror on, e.g. *magic, man, map, marmalade, mask, May, milk, million, minute, mirror, mistake, Monday, money, monkey, monster, month, morning, mouth, mum, music.*

- Children who are unable to think of a word may simply say *mirror*.
- Repeat the above activity, passing a newspaper and asking children to think of words beginning with *n*.

Guided/independent work

- Ask the children to think of an alliterative sentence using *m* or *n*, or recall one of the sentences composed during the shared writing session.
- Or they may like to use one of the ideas on pages 38 or 40 of Starter Level Big Book C. Help them to write out or copy their alliterative sentence and illustrate it.

Plenary

- Invite children to read their alliterative sentences to the rest of the class and show their illustrations.

DAY 4

Starter Level Big Book C pp. 38–41

Shared reading

- Re-read the dictionary pages on pages 38–41 of Starter Level Big Book C and ask the children the questions in the "To think and talk about" boxes.

Focused word/sentence work

- Give each child a lower case letter. Call letters out randomly, using letter names rather than sounds. The child with the corresponding letter is to run to the alphabet frieze (see Preparation) and hold it against the correct letter to show that they match.
- Repeat the above activity using upper case letters.

Guided/independent work

- Provide children, in pairs, with a selection of lower case letters and corresponding upper case letters (see Preparation). Set them the task of matching the upper and lower case letters.
- Children who complete this activity quickly could be set an extension task: to sequence the letters in alphabetical order.

Plenary

- Recite or sing the alphabet.
- Tell the class that there are 26 letters in the alphabet. Explain that there are 13 letters in the first half of the alphabet. Recite the alphabet again until you reach the thirteenth letter (*m*).
- Tell the children to think about the letter that begins their name. Ask those whose initial letter is in the first half of the alphabet to stand on one side of the room, and those whose initial letter is in the second half of the alphabet to stand on the other side of the room.
- Once the children have all made their decision and moved to the relevant side of the room, recite the alphabet again, pausing at *m*.

DAY 5

Starter Level Big Book C pp. 42–43; Skills Master 107

Shared reading

- If possible, show the class the end pages of some dictionaries and word books, e.g. word lists for colours, numbers, shapes, opposites, animals, etc. Talk about the different uses of these additional pages.

- Turn to pages 42 and 43 of Starter Level Big Book C. Explain that these pages are end pages from the same dictionary as the extracts on pages 38–41.

- Talk about what "opposite" means. See how many of the pictures the children can identify without reading the words. Where they are unable to identify pictures, read one of the words and see if they are able to work out the opposite (unless they are able to decode or recognise the words for themselves).

- Ask the questions in the "To think and talk about" box.

Focused word/sentence work

- Hand out your word cards from Set 1 (see Preparation) to a group of children. Hold each word in Set 2 up for the class to read, then invite the child holding the opposite word to show and read it to the class.

Guided/independent work

- Skills Master 107 focuses on opposite words.

Plenary

- Hand out your word cards from Set 2 (see Preparation) to a group of children. Hold each word in Set 1 up for the class to read, then invite the child holding the opposite word to show and read it to the class.

Consolidation and extension

- Skills Master 108 is a consolidation activity, focusing on CVC words beginning with *m*.

- Revisit the alphabet texts in Starter Level Big Book B, unit 17.

Unit 28 — The Gingerbread Man

Key Learning Objectives

TL4 To notice the difference between spoken and written forms through re-telling known stories

TL5 To understand how story book language works and to use some formal elements when re-telling stories, e.g. *"Once there was ... "*, *"She lived in a little ... "*; *"he replied ... "*

TL6 To re-read frequently a variety of familiar texts, e.g. big books, story books, taped stories with texts, own writing

TL7 To use knowledge of familiar texts to re-enact or re-tell to others, recounting the main points in correct sequence

TL8 To locate and read significant parts of the text, e.g. *"You can't catch me I'm the Gingerbread Man ... "*

TL9 To be aware of story structures, e.g. actions/reactions, consequences, and the ways that stories are built up and concluded

TL11 Through shared writing:
f) to apply knowledge of letter/sound correspondences in helping the teacher to scribe, and re-reading what the class has written

TL12 Through guided and independent writing:
d) to write sentences to match pictures or sequences of pictures

TL14 To use experience of stories as a basis for independent writing, e.g. re-telling, substitution, extension, and through shared composition with adults

WL2 Knowledge of grapheme/phoneme correspondences through:
a) hearing and identifying initial sounds in words
b) reading letter(s) that represent(s) the sound(s): *a, f, x*
c) writing each letter in response to each sound: *a, f, x*
d) identifying and writing initial and dominant phonemes in spoken words
e) identifying and writing initial and final phonemes in consonant-vowel-consonant (CVC) words

WL4 To link sound and spelling patterns by:
a) using knowledge of rhyme to identify families of rhyming CVC words
b) discriminating "onsets" from "rimes" in speech and spelling

WL6 To read on sight the 45 high frequency words to be taught by the end of YR

SL2 To use awareness of the grammar of a sentence to predict words during shared reading and when re-reading familiar stories

Range:	Story with predictable structure
Texts:	*The Gingerbread Man*, retold by Karina Law
Resources:	Starter Level Big Book C pp. 44–50
	Skills Masters 109–112 and 124 or 125
	Listen-along Cassette Track 20 and
	Read-along Book pp. 56–62

High frequency words

a, an, and, can, day, for, get, go, he, I, in, look, me, my, of, on, said, she, the, they, to, up, was, yes, you

Core activities

- Ask each child to re-read *The Gingerbread Man*, using the Listen-along Cassette (Track 20) and Read-along Book (pp. 56–62).
- Set up the role-play area to resemble the kitchen belonging to the old woman and man in *The Gingerbread Man*. Provide baking equipment, including a wooden or plastic rolling pin, a wooden spoon, a plastic bowl, and a simple "recipe" for the children to follow, so that they can pretend to make a gingerbread man and re-enact the early part of the story.
- Provide the children with props to re-enact the story of *The Gingerbread Man*.
- Ask each child to make the shapes *a* and *f* using modelling dough, a sand tray or finger paints.

Preparation

- Day 1: prepare word wheels or word slides (see Skills Master 124 or 125) for children to explore the rime -*an* using different onsets, e.g. *c, f, m, p, r, v*.
- Day 2: you will need an alphabet frieze positioned at a height that is accessible to the children.
- Day 3: enlarge a copy of Skills Master 110.
- Day 5: each pair of children will need plastic, foam or magnetic letters or letter cards for *b, f, i, m, o, s, x*.

DAY I

Starter Level Big Book C pp. 44–45;
Skills Master 124 or 125

Shared reading

- Read the title on page 44 of Starter Level Big Book C. How many children have heard this story before? Can they read the opening words ("Once upon a time ... ")?
- Read pages 44 and 45. How many children have tasted gingerbread? What did the old woman use to make the gingerbread man's eyes and mouth?
- Ask a child to point out the emboldened words spoken by the gingerbread man: "Run! Run! As fast as you can! You can't catch me, I'm the Gingerbread Man!" Ask the class to recite these words several times to memorise them.

Focused word/sentence work

- Re-read the gingerbread man's words on page 45. Ask the children to listen for two words that rhyme.

- Write the words *can* and *man* on the board. Read the last two lines on page 45. Can the children find another word that rhymes with *can* and *man*? (*ran*)

- Explore other words that rhyme with *can, man* and *ran*, e.g. *fan, Nan, pan, tan, van*. Help the children to discriminate the onset of each word.

Guided/independent work

- Using word wheels or word slides (see Skills Master 124 or 125), ask children to explore different onsets with the rime -*an*, and record the words they make.

Plenary

- Ask the children to recall the words they made using their word wheels or word slides. Prompt them to help you write these in a list on the board. Read and discuss them together.

DAY 2

Starter Level Big Book C pp. 46–50; Skills Master 109

Shared reading

- Ask the class to re-tell the beginning of the story of *The Gingerbread Man*. What do they think will happen next?

- Read the rest of the story on pages 46–50. Pause each time for the children to read the words spoken by the gingerbread man: "Run! Run! As fast as you can! You can't catch me, I'm the Gingerbread Man!"

- Ask the children to explain why the cow and the horse could not catch the gingerbread man. Can they explain how the fox managed to catch him?

Focused word/sentence work

- Look at page 50. Can the children find a word that is printed in capital letters? What does the word say and why is it printed in this way?

- Revise CVC words with the rime -*an* studied on Day 1.

- Focus on the medial vowel in *man, can* and *ran*. Demonstrate how to write the letter *a* on the board for the children to air trace and finger trace. Compare the upper and lower case letter shapes on an alphabet frieze.

- Think of words beginning with the short vowel *a*, e.g. *acrobat, ambulance, ant, arrow, astronaut*. Explain that although only a few words begin with this phoneme, it can be found in the middle of many other words.

- Ask the children to help you make a word chain of CVC words containing the letter *a* by listening carefully to each phoneme as you slowly say the words. Ask them to tell you the phonemes they can hear in the word *rat*. Write each letter on the board as the children correctly tell you each phoneme they hear.

- Ask them which letter they need to change to turn *rat* into *hat*. Which letters do they need to change to turn *hat* into *mat* and *mat* into *cat*? Carry on until the children have built the words *cap, tap, map, man, pan*, by changing one letter at a time.

Guided/independent work

- Skills Master 109 focuses on CVC words containing the medial vowel *a*.

Plenary

- Encourage the class to re-tell the story of *The Gingerbread Man*.

DAY 3

Skills Master 110

Shared writing

- Display your enlarged copy of Skills Master 110. Ask the children to use the pictures to re-tell the story of *The Gingerbread Man*. Can they "fill in the gaps"? For example, the meeting between the gingerbread man and the cow is not depicted. How did the gingerbread man come to be balancing on the fox?

- Decide together upon a sentence to accompany each picture. Help the class to re-read the sentences they have helped to compose.

Focused word/sentence work

- Ask the children to help you make another word chain of CVC words containing the letter *a* by listening carefully to each phoneme as you slowly say the words. Begin by asking them to tell you the phonemes they can hear in the word *man*. Write each letter on the board as the children correctly tell you each phoneme they hear.

- Ask them which letter they need to change to turn *man* into *van*. Which letters do they need to change to turn *van* into *fan* and *fan* into *fat*? Carry on until the children have built the words *hat, ham, sam*.

- Once the children have noticed that the last word is a name, point out that there is something wrong with it. See if they can tell you that the initial *s* should be a capital letter.

Guided/independent work

- Give each child a copy of Skills Master 110 to re-tell the story of *The Gingerbread Man* in their own words. Help them to organise their ideas into sentences.

Plenary

- Invite children to read out or re-tell the sentences they made up to go with the pictures on Skills Master 110.

DAY 4

Starter Level Big Book C pp. 44–50; Skills Master 111

Shared reading

- Re-read the story of *The Gingerbread Man* on pages 44–50. Encourage them to join in where possible, particularly with the emboldened text: "Run! Run! As fast as you can! You can't catch me, I'm the Gingerbread Man!"

Focused word/sentence work

- Can the children find a word that starts with the phoneme *f* on page 50? (*fox*) Ask them to think of other words that begin with *f*, e.g. *face, fairy, farm, February, film, finger, fire, fish, flower, fly, food, foot, football, fork, Friday, friend, frog, fruit, fun*. Give clues to some of these words if necessary. Write some of the words on the board, modelling the correct way to write the letter *f*. Ask the class to air trace the shape, then finger trace it on a nearby surface.

Guided/independent work

- Skills Master 111 focuses on words beginning with the letter *f*.

Plenary

- Ask the children to help you make a word chain of CVC words beginning with *f*, by listening carefully to each phoneme as you slowly say the words. Begin by asking them to tell you the phonemes they can hear in the word *fit*. Write each letter on the board as the children correctly tell you each phoneme they hear.
- Ask them which letter they need to change to turn *fit* into *fat*. Which letters do they need to change to turn *fat* into *fan* and *fan* into *fun*?

DAY 5

Starter Level Big Book C pp. 44–50

Shared reading

- Ask the class to help you, through role-play, to re-tell the story of *The Gingerbread Man*.

Focused word/sentence work

- Write the word *fox* on the board and ask the class to tell you the separate phonemes they can hear in it. Prompt the class to tell you how to change the word *fox* into *fix* by changing one letter, and *fix* into *fax*.

- Who has a fax machine at home? How many children have seen a message being sent or received by fax?
- Give the children clues to other words that contain *x* and write these on the board, e.g. *axe, box, exit, mix, ox, six, x-ray*.

Guided/independent work

- Give the children, in pairs, the letters *b, f, i, m, o, s, x* (see Preparation) to practise building CVC words ending in *x*.

Plenary

- Read the story of *The Gingerbread Man* on pages 44–50 of Starter Level Big Book C again.

Consolidation and extension

- Skills Master 112 features a word chain of CVC words containing the medial vowel *a*.
- Make edible gingerbread men and women, or decorative clay models.
- Read and compare different versions of The Gingerbread Man.

Unit 29 — Bears Everywhere

Key Learning Objectives

TL6	To re-read frequently a variety of familiar texts, e.g. big books, taped poems with texts, poems, information books, captions
TL10	To re-read and recite rhymes with predictable and repeated patterns
WL2	Knowledge of grapheme/phoneme correspondences through: a) hearing and identifying initial sounds in words b) reading letter(s) that represent(s) the sound(s): *b* c) writing each letter in response to each sound: *b* d) identifying and writing initial and dominant phonemes in spoken words
WL6	To read on sight the 45 high frequency words to be taught by the end of YR
WL9	To recognise the critical features of words, e.g. shape, length, and common spelling patterns
WL11	To make collections of personal interest or significant words and words linked to particular topics
SL2	To use awareness of the grammar of a sentence to predict words during shared reading and when re-reading familiar stories

Range:	Modern poetry with predictable structures and patterned language Simple non-fiction text
Texts:	*Algy Met a Bear*, Anon *All About Bears*, Karina Law *Here a Bear, There a Bear*, John Foster
Resources:	Starter Level Big Book C pp. 51–55 Skills Masters 113–116 and 121–123 Listen-along Cassette Track 21 and Read-along Book pp. 63–64

High frequency words

a, all, and, are, for, in, like, look, of, on, the, they, to, was

Core activities

- Give each child an opportunity to re-read *Here a Bear, There a Bear* by John Foster, using the Listen-along Cassette (Track 21) and Read-along Book (pp. 63–64).

- Using the pictures featured on Day 3, ask the children to match them to the sentences you printed out (see Shared writing).

- Provide modelling dough for the children to make a cake as they recite the nursery rhyme learned on Day 2 (Pat-a-cake, Pat-a-cake, Baker's man). Ask them to mark the cake with an upper case *B* for *Baby*.

- Ask all the children, in pairs, to sort out the items beginning with *b* and put them into the box labelled *b* (see Day 3).

Preparation

- Day 2: you will need the following high frequency flashcards, featured in Skills Masters 121–123: *a, all, and, are, for, in, like, look, of, on, the, they, to.*

  The children will need illustrated dictionaries and word books appropriate to their ability.

- Day 3: enlarge and cut out the three pictures on Skills Master 114 for whole class use.

  You will also need a large box labelled *b* and a collection of items, most of which begin with *b*, e.g. a bag, a ball, a balloon, a banana, a bandage, a bat, a battery, a bear, a bell, a book, a boot, a bowl, bread, a brush, a button.

  Prepare large word cards for whole class work featuring the following words: *Black, like, bears, honey, bamboo, Pandas, eat, live, on, Polar, land, icy.*

- Day 4: you will need a collection of teddy bears to help children complete sentences about bears in the plenary activity.

- Day 5: divide an A4 sheet into four sections and write the following words (one in each section): *bathroom, bedroom, sitting-room, kitchen*. Copy enough sheets for each pair of children and cut the words out in preparation for the children.

DAY 1

Starter Level Big Book C p. 51; Skills Master 113

Shared reading

- Introduce today's poem, *Algy Met a Bear*. Point to the word *Anon* and ask the children to tell you what the words under a poem usually tell you (the poet's name). Explain that this word is short for *Anonymous*, which means that we do not know who wrote this poem.

- What can the children see in the picture on page 51 of Starter Level Big Book C? Read the poem to them and ask them to explain what has happened to Algy (whose hat and shoes can be seen in the illustration).

- Teach the children to recite the poem, continuing to point to each word as you read together.

Focused word/sentence work

- Ask the children to tell you the phoneme they hear at the start of the word *bear*. Write the letter *b* on the board and ask the children to finger trace the shape in the air and on a nearby surface.

- Ask the children to think of more words that begin with *b*, e.g. *baby, back, badger, bag, ball, balloon, banana, bat, bed, bin, bit, bone, boot, box, boy, brush, bus*. Give them clues to some of these words if necessary.

- Ask the class to listen for another word beginning with *b* (*bulge*) as you recite *Algy Met a Bear* together once more.

Guided/independent work

- Skills Master 113 is a consolidation activity focusing on words beginning with *b*.

Plenary

- Recite together the poem you taught the class during today's shared reading session: *Algy Met a Bear*.

DAY 2

Starter Level Big Book C pp. 52–53; Skills Masters 121–123

Shared reading

- Open Starter Level Big Book C at pages 52 and 53. Ask the class to tell you what sort of text they think this will be. If they correctly guess that it is information text, ask them to explain why they think that. Help them to read the title of the non-fiction text.

- Can anyone identify any of the bears in the photographs? (Strictly speaking, pandas are not bears.) Read through the text on pages 52 and 53, prompting the children to read high frequency words and the key word *bears*.

- Ask the questions in the "To think and talk about" box.

Focused word/sentence work

- Ask the children to find two words beginning with *b* on page 52. Who can find a word, other than *bear*, beginning with *b* on page 53? (*bamboo*)

- Using flashcards featured in Skills Masters 121–123 (see Preparation), practise reading the following high frequency words: *a, all, and, are, for, in, like, look, of, on, the, they, to*. Challenge the children to find these words on pages 52–53.

Guided/independent work

- Ask the children to find things beginning with *b* using an illustrated dictionary or word book. More able children could draw and label some of the things they find. (You may like to provide them with a large outline of a bear in which to record the words.)

Plenary

- Recite the nursery rhyme, Pat-a-cake, Pat-a-cake, Baker's man:

  Pat-a-cake, pat-a-cake,
  Baker's man,
  Bake me a cake
  As fast as you can.
  Pat it and prick it
  And mark it with B,
  and put it in the oven
  For Baby and me.

- How many words can the children hear in this rhyme that begin with the letter *b*? (*baker, bake, baby*) Why is the cake marked with *B*?

DAY 3

Starter Level Big Book C, pp. 52–53; Skills Master 114

Shared writing

- Show the class your enlarged copies of the illustrations on Skills Master 114. Which types of bears are shown?

- Taking each picture in turn, ask the class to tell you what they remember about the bear. Then compare with the information given on pages 52 and 53.

- Taking direction from the children, write one sentence to go with each picture. Then read them together, while three children hold up the pictures; ask the class to tell you which of the pictures goes with each sentence.

- Keep the pictures used during this session; you will also need to word process the three sentences composed by the class and print them out for one of the core activities.

Focused word/sentence work

- Using your collection of items (see Preparation), ask the class to help you sort out the items beginning with *b* and put them into the box labelled *b*.

Guided/independent work

- Skills Master 114 requires children to sequence words to complete three sentences. Once completed, the page will resemble a non-fiction page. If possible, provide children with flashcards featuring the given words so that they can move them around on a desktop.

Plenary

- Choose one of the sentences featured on Skills Master 114 and give a group of children the corresponding words (see Preparation).

- Ask the children to stand at the front of the class holding the words. Ask the rest of the class to help move the children into the right positions in order to construct a sentence about a bear. Repeat for the two remaining sentences.

DAY 4

Starter Level Big Book C pp. 54–55; Skills Master 115

Shared reading

- Introduce the poem *Here a Bear, There a Bear* by John Foster, which begins on page 54. Are the children able to recognise the repeated word *bear* in the title?

- Talk about the pictures. What are the bears doing in each illustration? Read pages 54 and 55, pausing for the children to supply the words *bear* and *bears*. Ask the questions in the "To think and talk about" box.

Focused word/sentence work

- Who can spot the difference between the words *bear* and *bears*? Why is there an *s* at the end of the word *bears*?

- Re-read the poem, pausing for the children to supply the rhyming words *chairs, jelly, squash, floors* and *everywhere*.

- Write the prepositions *in, on* and *under* on the board for the children to read. Look around the classroom for ways of demonstrating these words and question the children accordingly, e.g. "Where are the fish?" (*in the tank*); "Where are the dustpan and brush?" (*under the sink*)

Guided/independent work

- Skills Master 115 requires children to match phrases and pictures based on today's shared reading text. The high frequency preposition words *in* and *on* are reinforced.

Plenary

- Write the following sentence openers on the board.

    My bear's name is ...
    He likes to eat ...
    He likes to play with ...

- Ask the children to think of ways to complete the sentences using words beginning with *b*. For example, *Ben, bananas, balloons; Betty, biscuits, bats and balls; Bella, bacon, books.*

DAY 5

Starter Level Big Book C pp. 54–55

Shared reading

- Re-read the poem *Here a Bear, There a Bear* by John Foster, on pages 54 and 55.

Focused word/sentence work

- Hand out a set of word cards to each pair of children (see Preparation). Take one set and hold up each word in turn until the children are familiar with them. Point out that *bathroom, bedroom* and *sitting-room* each end in *room*.

- How many children have a sitting room at home? How many children call this room something else, e.g. *lounge, front room*. Note that *bathroom* and *bedroom* share the same initial phoneme.

- Ask the children, in pairs, to hold two of the words each. Ask the class questions relating to the words, and ask the children holding the relevant word card to hold it in the air. For example, "Which room would you find a fridge in?"; "Which room do you sleep in?"; "Which room might you watch the television in?"

- Be aware that some children may have televisions in their bedrooms and, perhaps, the kitchen.

Guided/independent work

- Using the sentence openers you worked on during the plenary session on Day 4, ask children to copy the words (or provide them with a writing frame) and complete the sentences for a real or imaginary bear.

Plenary

- Repeat the word game you played during today's focused word/sentence work session.

Consolidation and extension

- Skills Master 116 requires children to match pictures, showing bears engaged in different activities, to the corresponding sentences.

- Teach the class to recite the poem *Here a Bear, There a Bear* by John Foster, from memory.

- Make a lift-the-flap book. Each child could contribute one page, depicting a bear in a different hiding place. A small flap could be attached over the bear in its hiding place and a caption could be added underneath the picture.

- Make a collection of other poems and stories about bears, e.g. Goldilocks and the Three Bears.

- Make a collection of bears in the role-play area. Position the bears in different places, e.g. on a chair, under a table, and use them to reinforce prepositions.

- Make a class poem about bears using the format established by John Foster in *Here a Bear, There a Bear*. For example:

    Here a bear, there a bear.
    Everywhere there's a bear.
    Bears in the classroom
    Bears in the hall
    Bears on the climbing frame ...

Unit 30 — Where's Tim's Ted?

Key Learning Objectives

TL7	To use knowledge of familiar texts to re-enact or re-tell to others, recounting the main points in correct sequence
TL9	To be aware of story structures, e.g. actions/reactions, consequences, and the ways that stories are built up and concluded
TL10	To re-read and recite stories and rhymes with predictable and repeated patterns and experiment with similar rhyming patterns
TL14	To use experience of stories, poems and simple recounts as a basis for independent writing
WL1	To understand and be able to rhyme through: a) recognising, exploring and working with rhyming patterns b) extending these patterns by analogy, generating new and invented words in speech and spelling
WL2	Knowledge of grapheme/phoneme correspondences through: a) hearing and identifying initial sounds in words b) reading letter(s) that represent(s) the sound(s): *i, sh* c) writing each letter in response to each sound: *i, sh* d) identifying and writing initial and dominant phonemes in spoken words e) identifying and writing initial and final phonemes in consonant-vowel-consonant (CVC) words
WL4	To link sound and spelling patterns by: a) using knowledge of rhyme to identify families of rhyming CVC words c) identifying alliteration in known and new and invented words
WL5	To read on sight a range of familiar words
WL6	To read on sight the 45 high frequency words to be taught by the end of YR

Range:	Story with predictable structure and patterned language
Texts:	From *Where's Tim's Ted?*, Ian Whybrow and Russell Ayto, Collins
Resources:	Starter Level Big Book C pp. 56–64 Skills Masters 117–120

High frequency words

a, all, and, big, can, come, for, go, he, I, in, is, it, look, me, my, no, of, on, see, the, they, this, to, you

Core activities

- Provide the children with props to re-enact the story extract from *Where's Tim's Ted?* including a teddy bear, and a variety of toy farm animals.
- Provide different invitation templates in the writing corner for children to complete. More able children may use the sample invitations as models for designing their own invitations.

- Ask the children to make shopping lists for a teddy bears' picnic.
- Set up the role-play area for a picnic. Provide a rug, plastic cups, plates and cutlery, etc. Allow children to bring their teddy bears into school to take part.

Preparation

- Day 2: each pair of children will need the following plastic, foam or magnetic letters or letter cards: *b, d, f, g, i, m, p, s* and *x*.
- Day 3: prepare the following word cards: *Tim, Ted, pig, Ben, red, shed, hen, pen, then, big, dim, him, bed, fed, wig, dig, den, men, ten.*

DAY 1

Starter Level Big Book C pp. 56–59; Skills Master 117

Shared reading

- Introduce the story extract *Where's Tim's Ted?* by Ian Whybrow, which begins on page 56 of Starter Level Big Book C. Help the children to read the title.
- Write the name *Tim* on the board to familiarise the children with the word.
- Talk about the pictures on pages 56 and 57. What is happening on page 57? What are the characters looking for (refer back to the title)? What do they think the little boy's name is?
- Read pages 56 to 59, pointing to the words as you do so, but without pausing for the children to join in. (Try to keep the rhythm of the text flowing.) What do the children think will happen next? Ask them to make suggestions as to where Tim's Ted might be.

Focused word/sentence work

- Focus on the medial vowel in *Tim*. Demonstrate how to write the letter *i* on the board for the children to air trace and finger trace.
- Compare the upper and lower case letter shapes on an alphabet frieze.
- Think of words beginning with the short vowel *i*, e.g. *if, ill, imagination, in, ink, information, insect, instruction, invisible, is, it*. Explain that although only a few words begin with this phoneme, it can be found in the middle of many other words.
- Ask the children to help you make a word chain of CVC words containing the letter *i* by listening carefully to each phoneme as you slowly say the words. Ask them to tell you the phonemes they can hear in the word *win*. Write each letter on the board as the children correctly tell you each phoneme they hear.
- Ask them which letter they need to change to turn *win* into *fin, fin* into *fix* and *fix* into *mix*? Carry on until the children have built the words *six, sit, pit, pig*, by changing one letter at a time.

Guided/independent work

- Skills Master 117 focuses on CVC words with medial short vowel *i*.

Plenary

- Re-read pages 56–59 of Starter Level Big Book C, emphasising the rhyming words: *moon/soon*; *Red/Ted*; *chairs/upstairs*; *night/right*; *sight/moonlight*; *Gruff/enough*.

- Draw the children's attention to the speech bubbles on pages 57 and 59. Can the children recall Tim's words in each instance?

DAY 2

Starter Level Big Book C pp. 56–64

Shared reading

- Turn to pages 56 and 57 of Starter Level Big Book C. Ask the children to recall the opening section of the story. Re-read page 59, pointing to each word in turn, and focusing on the different presentation devices.

- Continue reading the story extract to the end of page 64 without breaking the flow of the text. Talk about the story with the class.

- Ask the questions in the "To think and talk about" box. What are the names of the dog and the horse? (*Ben* and *Pacer*)

Focused word/sentence work

- Ask the children to help you make another word chain of CVC words containing the letter *i* by listening carefully to each phoneme as you slowly say the words. Invite a child to write the word *pig* on the board.

- Ask the class which letter they need to change to turn *pig* into *wig* and *wig* into *big*. Carry on until the children have built the words *bin*, *tin*, and *tim*, by changing one letter at a time.

- Once the children have noticed that the last word is the name of the character in this unit's shared text, point out that there is something wrong with it. See if they can tell you that the initial *t* should be a capital letter.

Guided/independent work

- Give the children, in pairs, the letters *b*, *d*, *f*, *g*, *i*, *m*, *p*, *s* and *x* (see Preparation) to practise building CVC words with the medial vowel *i*.

Plenary

- Look through the extract from *Where's Tim's Ted?*, focusing on some of the presentation features, such as speech marks and the use of capital letters.

- Talk about the illustrations. Which of the animal characters do the children like best? Look closely at Tim's duvet cover and curtains on page 58. Can the children spot the details?

DAY 3

Skills Master 118

Shared writing

- Explain to the class that you will be holding a teddy bears' picnic at the end of the week. Ask them to help you write an invitation that could be sent to their own teddy bears. For example:

> Dear Ted
>
> Please come to our picnic on Friday 3rd July, at St Dunstan's School Garden.
>
> There will be lots of food and games to play.
>
> Love from
> Edward

Focused word/sentence work

- Hand out the following word cards, featuring characters from the shared text (see Preparation), to different children and ask them: "Tim", "Ted", "pig" and "Ben" to stand at the front of the class.

- Hold up the remaining word cards, one at a time, and ask the class to read them and decide which of the four character names they rhyme with. Once everyone is agreed, give the card to the relevant child.

- Once all the cards are with the four children at the front of the class, read them together in their rhyming groups.

Guided/independent work

- Skills Master 118 features an invitation to a teddy bears' picnic which may be completed (adding the date, location and name of child) and taken home to give to a child's favourite teddy bear. More able children might like to design invitations of their own.

- Children could then bring their teddy bears in for a picnic at an agreed time. This would provide speaking and listening and role-play opportunities, as well as an excellent stimulus for writing a recount of the event.

Plenary

- Repeat the rhyming game you played during today's focused word/sentence work session.

DAY 4

Starter Level Big Book C pp. 56–64; Skills Master 119

Shared reading

- Re-read the whole of the story extract from *Where's Tim's Ted?* on pages 56–64. Encourage the children to join in where possible, but try not to break the rhythm of the text.

Focused word/sentence work

- Look at the speech bubble on page 59. Read Tim's words, placing emphasis on *Ssshhh*. Write the letters *sh* on the board and ask the children to tell you the phoneme that these letters make.

- Ask the children to raise their hands when they hear this phoneme as you read page 60 (*flashlight, shed, Ssshhh-ssshhh*). Repeat this task for page 62 (*sheep, SSSHHH*).

- Encourage the children to think of other words that begin with *sh*, e.g. *shell, ship, shoes, shop*.

- Give clues to words that end with *sh*. For example, "something you use to make your hair neat" (*brush*); "an animal that lives in water" (*fish*). Ask the children to think of words that rhyme with *fish*, e.g. *dish, wish*.

Guided/independent work

- Skills Master 119 requires children to spell rhyming words containing the phoneme *sh*.

Plenary

- Recite alliterative tongue twisters using *sh* such as "She sells sea shells on the seashore." Make up more *sh* tongue twisters of your own.

DAY 5

Starter Level Big Book C pp. 56–64

Shared reading

- Re-read the whole of the story extract from *Where's Tim's Ted?* on pages 56–64. Let the children experiment with different voices for the animals.

Focused word/sentence work

- Focus on the alliteration in the phrase *Tim's Ted*. Make up alliterative titles for other stories, using the names of children in your class, e.g. "Harry's Hat", "Kiran's Kite", "Francesca's flower".

Guided/independent work

- Help the children to write simple sentences about *Where's Tim's Ted?* For example, "Tim has a dog called Ben."; "Mummy pig had Ted." More able children may want to attempt to re-tell the story extract in their own words.

Plenary

- Invite children to read their sentences to the rest of the class.

Consolidation and extension

- Skills Master 120 is a cloze activity, featuring high frequency words, prepositions and CVC words.

- Read *Where's Tim's Ted?* by Ian Whybrow in its entirety to find out if Tim and his Ted return safely to bed.

- Take time to review all three Starter Level Big Books that the children have studied this academic year. Flick through the pages to see which poems, stories and non-fiction texts the children recall reading.

- Ask the children to talk about their favourite stories and poems, giving reasons for their choices. Choose a few class favourites to revisit during the next week.

Copymasters

WELL DONE!

Focus on Literacy Starter Level
ACHIEVEMENT AWARD

Awarded to _____

For _____

Signed _____ Date _____

School _____

WELL DONE!

Focus on Literacy Starter Level
ACHIEVEMENT AWARD

Awarded to _____

For _____

Signed _____ Date _____

School _____

Starter Level

Word level work: phonics, spelling, vocabulary

Objective	Comment
Phonological awareness, phonics and spelling	
1 Ability to rhyme	
2 Knowledge of grapheme/phoneme correspondences	
3 Alphabetic and phonic knowledge	
4 Ability to link sound and spelling patterns	
Word recognition, graphic knowledge and spelling	
5 Reading on sight familiar words	
6 Reading on sight 45 high frequency words	
7 Reading on sight words from texts of appropriate difficulty	
8 Reading and writing own name	
9 Recognising the critical features of words	
Vocabulary extension	
10 Learning new words	
11 Making collections of words linked to particular topics	
Handwriting	
12 Developing pencil grip	
13 Producing a controlled line	
14 Writing letters using the correct sequence of movements	

Sentence level work: grammar and punctuation

Objective	Comment
Grammatical awareness	
1 Checking for sense	
2 Drawing on grammatical awareness	
3 Knowing that words are ordered left to right and need to be read that way to make sense	
4 Using a capital letter for the start of own name	

Text level work: comprehension and composition

Objective	Comment
Reading	
Understanding of print	
1 Recognising printed and handwritten words and making correspondences between written and spoken words	
Reading comprehension	
2 Using a variety of cues when reading	
3 Reading unfamiliar words	
4 Noticing the difference between spoken and written forms	
5 Understanding story book language	
6 Re-reading familiar texts	
7 Re-enacting familiar texts	
8 Locating and reading significant parts of text	
9 Awareness of story structures	
10 Re-reading and reciting stories and rhymes with predictable and repeated patterns	
Writing	
Understanding of print	
11 Understanding how writing is formed and that it can be used for a range of purposes	
Composition	
12 Experimenting with writing	
13 Thinking about and discussing writing intentions	
14 Using experience of stories, poems and simple recounts as a basis for independent writing	
15 Using writing to communicate in a variety of ways	

Appendices

Focus on *Literacy* and the Scottish 5–14 Guidelines (pre-Level A – Level A)

Introduction to 5–14 Guidelines	5–14 Guidelines	Unit 1	2	3	4	5	6	7	8	9	10
Listening											
• Pay attention to information and instructions from an adult	• Listening for information, instructions and directions						✓				
• Learn not to interrupt others in the group	• Listening in groups	✓									
• Learn to take part in discussion activities											
• Encouraged to respond and comment on what interests them	• Listening in order to respond to texts	✓	✓	✓		✓		✓	✓	✓	✓
	• Awareness of genre	✓			✓						
Talking											
• Use language for a variety of purposes	• Conveying information, instructions and directions										
• Learn to take turns, listening to other speakers	• Talking in groups				✓					✓	
• Use talk in play to arrive at outcomes	• Talk about experiences, feelings and opinions	✓	✓	✓		✓				✓	✓
• Re-tell a story or rhyme in play	• Talk about texts	✓	✓		✓	✓	✓	✓		✓	✓
	• Audience awareness										
Reading											
• Develop an understanding of the purposes of print by reading labels, signs and captions	• Reading for information			✓	✓		✓	✓	✓		
• Be involved in pre-reading activities to develop skills of matching, discrimination, left to right eye movement and sequencing											
• Learn an initial sight vocabulary (common words)	• Reading for enjoyment	✓	✓	✓	✓	✓		✓	✓	✓	✓
• Develop phonic (including onset and rime and blending) skills and skills of word attack											
• Learn to enjoy books by listening to stories and poems and talking about them	• Reading to reflect on the writer's craft										
• Learn to recognise the common genres in fiction and non-fiction	• Awareness of genre	✓		✓	✓			✓	✓		
• Recognise and read aloud familiar words	• Reading aloud	✓	✓	✓		✓	✓	✓	✓	✓	
• Learn language terms	• Knowledge about language	✓	✓	✓	✓	✓	✓	✓	✓		✓
• Understand first letter order											
Writing											
• With teacher support, observe, select important features and order their writing	• Functional writing	✓		✓	✓		✓	✓			
	• Personal writing				✓					✓	
• Understand the writing purpose	• Imaginative writing	✓	✓	✓	✓						✓
• Begin to understand when to use capital letters and full stops	• Punctuation and structure	✓				✓	✓				
• Practise sequencing simple stories and events											
• Have an awareness of letter sequence	• Spelling	✓	✓	✓	✓	✓	✓	✓	✓	✓	
• Form letters and space words legibly	• Handwriting and presentation	✓	✓							✓	✓
	• Knowledge about language	✓	✓							✓	

High frequency words
to be taught as sight recognition
words through Reception Year

11	12	13	14	15	16	17	18	19	20	21	22	23	24	25	26	27	28	29	30
		✓	✓	✓	✓	✓		✓	✓	✓	✓	✓	✓	✓	✓	✓	✓	✓	
														✓		✓			
✓	✓	✓	✓	✓	✓			✓	✓		✓							✓	✓
		✓																✓	
											✓		✓						
										✓						✓			
✓	✓	✓	✓		✓	✓	✓	✓	✓		✓	✓	✓	✓			✓	✓	✓
✓	✓	✓	✓	✓	✓	✓	✓	✓	✓	✓	✓	✓	✓	✓		✓	✓	✓	✓
													✓						
			✓	✓	✓	✓			✓		✓				✓	✓		✓	
✓	✓	✓	✓	✓			✓	✓		✓		✓	✓	✓			✓	✓	✓
		✓					✓			✓							✓		✓
										✓			✓		✓		✓		
✓	✓	✓	✓	✓	✓	✓	✓	✓	✓	✓	✓	✓	✓	✓	✓	✓	✓	✓	✓
			✓	✓	✓	✓	✓	✓	✓	✓	✓	✓	✓	✓	✓	✓	✓	✓	✓
	✓				✓	✓				✓	✓			✓				✓	✓
	✓						✓	✓		✓			✓						
✓		✓	✓		✓			✓		✓	✓		✓			✓			
							✓			✓	✓						✓		✓
✓	✓	✓	✓	✓	✓	✓	✓	✓	✓	✓	✓	✓	✓	✓	✓	✓	✓	✓	✓
✓	✓	✓		✓	✓	✓	✓	✓	✓	✓	✓	✓	✓		✓	✓	✓	✓	✓
										✓									

High frequency words to be taught as 'sight recognition' words through Reception Year

a	get	on
all	go	play
am	going	said
and	he	see
are	I	she
at	in	the
away	is	they
big	it	this
can	like	to
cat	look	up
come	me	was
dad	mum	we
day	my	went
dog	no	yes
for	of	you